CONTENTS

To the Student

Welcome to *At Work in the U.S.* This book has stories about Maria, Ana, Joe, and Ramón. They came to live and work in the U.S. Their stories and the stories of others will help you better understand the U.S. workplace. This book will also help you build the vocabulary and communication skills you need at work.

At Work in the U.S. is divided into four units. Each unit is centered on a work-related theme. The themes are *job information*, *job benefits*, *safety*, and *workplace culture*. The stories are set in many places where people work—hospitals, hotels, kitchens, factories, stores, nursing homes, construction sites, and others.

There are four chapters in each unit. The chapters include exercises in
- vocabulary
- reading
- grammar
- listening
- pronunciation and dialogues
- writing

Chapters also include the opportunity to
- share your culture and learn about others
- talk about problems
- apply what you have learned to your job

At Work in the U.S. contains a variety of exercises to help you set goals and evaluate your progress at work. You will also practice the skills you need to do a better job.

At Work in the U.S.

Readings and Language for Job Success

Paula M. Jablon • *Ellen E. Vacco*

New Readers Press

At Work in the U.S.
ISBN 978-1-56420-393-9

Copyright © 2003 New Readers Press
New Readers Press
ProLiteracy's Publishing Division
104 Marcellus Street, Syracuse, New York 13204
www.newreaderspress.com

Printed in the United States of America
19   18   17   16   15   14

Proceeds from the sale of New Readers Press materials support professional
development, training, and technical assistance programs of ProLiteracy
that benefit local literacy programs in the U.S. and around the globe.

Acquisitions Editor: Paula L. Schlusberg
Content Editor: Judi Lauber
Copy Editor: Marcia Hough
Production Director: Heather Witt
Designer: Kimbrly Koennecke
Illustrations: Carolyn Boehmer, Len Shalansky
Production Specialist: Debbie Christiansen
Cover Design: Andrea Woodbury

AT WORK IN THE U.S.

This book is about a family.
They came to the U.S. to stay.
They wanted to get good jobs
and live a better way.

Joe is married to Maria.
Her sister, Ana, lives near
with Ramón and their children.
They help each other here.

They all have different jobs
and try to do their best.
Now read about what they do
at work in the U.S.

UNIT 1
Maria's Story

Personal Information

LESSON 1
In the U.S.

Maria's Story

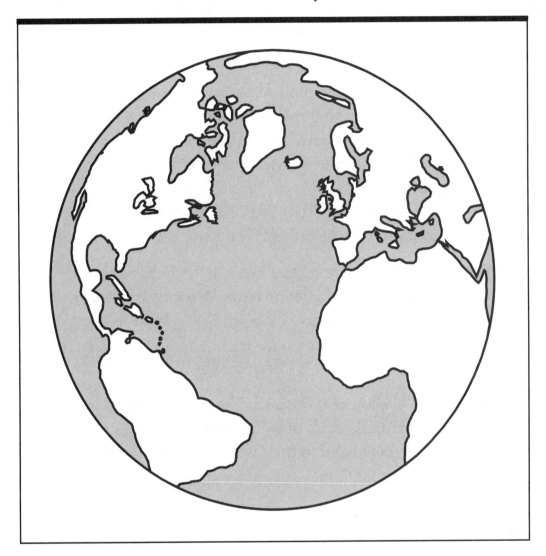

What country do you come from? Where do you live now?
Is it hard to live in a new country? What is hard for you?

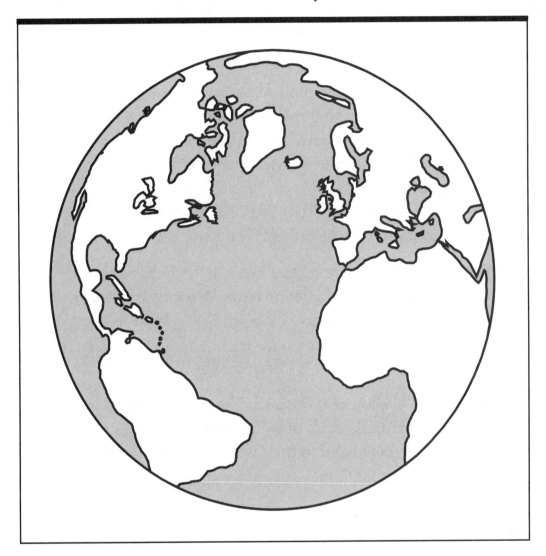 **Words for Work**

apartment	language
children	last name
city	married
first name	native country
hospital	nurse

More Words

different	neighbor
education	nervous
family	
friend	
important	

Hi! My name is Maria Garcia. Maria is my first name. My last name is Garcia. I come from Mexico. I am 38 years old. I am married. My husband's name is Joe. We have three children.

My family and I came to the United States three years ago. Now we live at 353 South Street in Boston, Massachusetts. Boston is a very big and beautiful city. We live in an apartment. It is small, but it is OK for now. My sister and her family live near us. My sister's name is Ana. Her husband's name is Ramón. They have two children. We also have many friends and nice neighbors. We help them. They help us.

Most of the time we are happy to be in the U.S. But it is not always easy. It is very different here. We miss our native country. It is hard to find a good job here. We have to learn the language. In Mexico I was a nurse. I cannot work as a nurse in the U.S. My English is not good yet.

I work in the kitchen of a hospital. There is an English as a Second Language (ESL) class at work. It begins on Thursday. I am very nervous, but I need to go. I want to learn more English. Education is important to me.

Comprehension

Circle *yes* or *no* after each sentence.

1. Maria's last name is Garcia.   yes   no

2. She is 28 years old.   yes   no

3. She lives in New York City.   yes   no

4. Maria and her family miss their country.   yes   no

5. Maria wants to learn more English.   yes   no

6. The ESL class begins on Tuesday.   yes   no

Vocabulary

A. Complete each sentence with one of these words or phrases.

apartment	family	language	native country
city	hospital	last name	nervous

1. Maria and her _____ came to the U.S. three years ago.

2. In the U.S. your _____ is your family name.

3. Boston is a big _____ .

4. Maria lives in a small _____ in Boston.

5. Doctors and nurses work in a _____ .

6. Mexico is Maria and Joe's _____ .

7. Maria is very _____ about going to ESL classes.

8. English is a hard _____ to learn.

B. Find and circle the words. Some words go across. Some words go down.

```
v  c  l  a  s  j  y  c  b  o        apartment
f  i  r  s  t  p  u  o  n  e        city
r  t  f  g  a  s  p  u  x  d        country
i  y  a  d  e  e  r  n  o  u        education
e  s  m  a  l  o  h  t  a  c        family
n  e  i  g  h  b  o  r  m  a        first
d  o  l  a  s  t  m  y  a  t        friend
c  r  y  n  j  a  r  s  o  i        last
a  m  a  r  r  i  e  d  b  o        married
a  p  a  r  t  m  e  n  t  n        neighbor
```

Language Skills

Present Tense with *Be*							
Full Form		**Contraction**		**Full Form**		**Contraction**	
I	am	(I'm)		we	are	(we're)	
you	are	(you're)		you	are	(you're)	
he		(he's)					
she }	is	(she's)		they	are	(they're)	
it		(it's)					

A. Complete each sentence with the correct verb form.

<table>
<tr><td>

Use the full form.

Example: He <u>is</u> my brother

1. I _____ 33 years old.

2. They _____ my neighbors.

3. She _____ very nervous.

4. You _____ late for work.

5. It _____ hard to find a good job.

</td><td>

Use the contraction.

Example: <u>He's</u> my brother

1. I _____ 33 years old.

2. They _____ my neighbors.

3. She _____ very nervous.

4. You _____ late for work.

5. It _____ hard to find a good job.

</td></tr>
</table>

Questions with *Be*			
Am	I	Are	we
Are	you	Are	you
	he		
Is {	she	Are	they
	it		

B. Complete the questions with the correct verb form.

Example: <u>Is</u> he your brother?

1. _____ you happy?

2. _____ Maria married?

3. _____ New York a big city?

4. _____ the apartment small?

5. _____ your children in school?

6. _____ they your friends?

10 Lesson 1

C. Make a question from each of the following sentences.

Example: They are neighbors.   Are they neighbors?

1. He is thirteen years old.   _____ ?

2. You are nervous.   _____ ?

3. She is a good worker.   _____ ?

4. You are from El Salvador.   _____ ?

5. It is Thursday.   _____ ?

6. Your children are in school.   _____ ?

🎧 Oral Practice: Pronunciation

A. Practice the two sounds of the letters *th*. Say the following words.

thank	thirteen	three		that	these
bathroom	everything	something		another	mother
both	north	tooth		the	they
think	thirty	Thursday		brother	other
birthday	nothing	with		there	this
month	tenth			father	together
				with	

Do you know other words with *th*?

B. Practice these sentences. Then say them as fast as you can.

1. Is Thanksgiving the third Thursday in the month of November?

2. There are thirteen bathrooms on the thirty-third floor.

🎧 Oral Practice: Dialogue

Answer the questions. Practice the dialogue with a partner.

Example: **A.** *What is your first name?* **A.** *What is your last name?*
 B. *My first name is Maria.* **B.** *My last name is Garcia.*
 A. *Please spell that.* **A.** *Please spell that.*
 B. <u>M A R I A</u> **B.** <u>G A R C I A</u>

A. What is your first name?

B. My first name is _____ .

A. Please spell that.

B. _ _ _ _ _ _ _ _ _ _ _ _ _ _ _ _ _ _ _

A. What is your last name?

B. My last name is _____ .

A. Please spell that.

B. _ _ _ _ _ _ _ _ _ _ _ _ _ _ _ _ _ _ _

A. What is your address?

B. My address is _____ .

A. Please spell the name of your street.

B. _ _ _ _ _ _ _ _ _ _ _ _ _ _ _ _ _ _ _

A. Please spell your city or town.

B. _ _ _ _ _ _ _ _ _ _ _ _ _ _ _ _ _ _ _

A. What country are you from?

B. I am from _____ .

A. When is your ESL class?

B. My class is on _____ .

Reading Practice

 **Read about Maria.**

Now I'm in the U.S.
It's not easy living here.
But I have my family
and some friends living near.

Things are very different here—
language, food, and more.
I work at my new job each day.
I work from 8 to 4.

There is an ESL class.
It starts sometime next week.
There is so much I have to learn—
to read and write and speak.

Discussion

1. When did you come to the U.S.? Was it hard for you?
   What is different here?
2. What was your job in your native country? What was your
   first job in the U.S.?

Application

Write about yourself. Share your story with your class.

My first name is _____ . My last name is

_____ . I come from _____ .

Now I live in _____ . My ESL class is on

_____ .

LESSON 2
At ESL Class

Maria's Story

NAME   Garcia   Maria   S.
          Last   First   Middle Initial

ADDRESS   353   South St.   566
        No.   Street   Apt. No.

      Boston   MA   02134
      City   State   Zip Code

TEL. NO. (617) 268-9877   SOC. SEC. NO. 097-75-8583
     Area Code

EMERGENCY NO. (617) 268-3200
          Area Code

SEX   MARITAL STATUS

☐ Male   ☒ Married

☒ Female   ☐ Single

DATE OF BIRTH 12 / 1 / 64
           Mo. Day Yr.

EMPLOYER County Hospital

SIGNATURE *Maria S. Garcia*   DATE 12/19/02

Do you fill out forms? Where do you fill out forms?
What kind of forms do you fill out?
Are forms hard for you to understand? Do you need help?

🎧 Words for Work

date of birth	female	print
emergency	form	signature
employee	male	single
employer	middle initial	Social Security number

🎧 More Words

afraid
explain
information
practice

Today is Thursday. It is the first day of ESL class. There are 15 students in the class. We are all employees at the hospital. Everyone is nervous. But we all need English for our jobs. We know it is important to study hard.

Our teacher's name is Ms. Jones. She gives each student a form to fill out. This is good for me. I sometimes have to fill out forms. I always need help. On this form, I have to print my name, address, telephone number, date of birth, Social Security number, and other information. A few of the students don't understand the words *middle initial*. I don't understand the words *single*, *male*, and *female*. Ms. Jones explains. She also teaches us how to say the words *emergency*, *signature*, and *employer*. We practice these words together.

Ms. Jones tells the class about herself. She asks us to call her Cathy. Then we all say our names. We talk a little bit about our native countries, families, and jobs. This is not easy for us. We only know a little English. Nobody wants to speak first. I am happy because I am not first. I don't like to speak English. I am afraid people will not understand me. But in class I have to try. I want to learn more English.

Comprehension

Circle *yes* or *no* after each sentence.

1. There are 13 students in the ESL class.   yes   no

2. All the students are nervous.   yes   no

3. The teacher's name is Ms. Smith.   yes   no

4. The students fill out forms.   yes   no

5. Maria does not understand all the words on the form.   yes   no

6. Everyone in the class speaks English very well.   yes   no

7. Maria likes to speak English.   yes   no

Vocabulary

A. Complete each sentence with one of these words.

emergency	female	male	signature
employer	form	print	single

1. On the first day of class, Maria has to fill out a _____ .

2. A woman is a _____ .

3. You are not married. You are _____ .

4. Your _____ is the company where you work.

5. A man is a _____ .

6. Your written name is your _____ .

7. Maria gets sick at work. Her boss calls her _____ telephone number.

8. You fill out a form. It is important to _____ the information.

B. Circle the word that does not belong.

Example: nervous   happy   afraid   (form)

1. first name   area code   middle initial   last name

2. city   children   street   apartment number

3. Social Security number   date of birth   native country   print

4. family   neighbors   emergency   friends

5. zip code   city   signature   state

6. address   class   students   teacher

Language Skills

Present Tense Negative of *Be*					
Full Form		**Contraction**	**Full Form**		**Contraction**
I	am not	(I'm not)	we	are not	(we aren't)
you	are not	(you aren't)	you	are not	(you aren't)
he		(he isn't)			
she }	is not	(she isn't)	they	are not	(they aren't)
it		(it isn't)			

A. Complete each sentence.

<u>Use the full form.</u>

Example: My job <u>is</u> <u>not</u> easy.

1. I _____ _____ a student.
2. She _____ _____ married.
3. Maria and Joe _____ _____ happy.
4. It _____ _____ Tuesday.
5. Ms. Jones _____ _____ a nurse.

<u>Use the contraction.</u>

Example: My job <u>isn't</u> easy.

1. I' _____ _____ a student.
2. She _____ married.
3. Maria and Joe _____ happy.
4. It _____ Tuesday.
5. Ms. Jones _____ a nurse.

B. Answer the questions in the negative. Use the correct contraction.

Examples: Are you married? <u>No, I'm not.</u>   Is he your neighbor? <u>No, he isn't.</u>

1. Is Ms. Jones a student? _____

2. Are you a child? _____

3. Are Maria and Joe in Mexico? _____

4. Is Boston a small city? _____

5. Are you an English teacher? _____

🎧 Oral Practice: Pronunciation

Dividing a word into parts helps you read it and say it. Practice dividing words into parts. Say the following words. Then say the parts. Finally, repeat the words.

Examples: important   im por tant   important   *security   se cur i ty   security

1. city	ci ty	city
2. country	coun try	country
3. happy	hap py	happy
4. form	form	form
5. easy	ea sy	easy
6. hospital	hos pi tal	hospital
7. study	stu dy	study
8. first	first	first
9. thirty	thir ty	thirty
10. only	on ly	only
11. emergency	e mer gen cy	emergency
12. very	ver y	very
13. name	name	name
14. family	fa mi ly	family
15. telephone	te le phone	telephone

*Note: The letter *y* at the end of some words sounds like the letter *e* as in *she*. Remember to pronounce it clearly.

Writing Practice

Complete the following form with personal information.
Please print.

PLEASE PRINT

_____

NAME _____
                  Last   First   Middle Initial

ADDRESS _____
                No.   Street   Apt. No.

                  _____
                City   State   Zip Code

TEL. NO. (_____) _____ SOC. SEC. NO. _____
        Area Code

EMERGENCY NO. (_____) _____
               Area Code

SEX   MARITAL STATUS

☐ Male   ☐ Married

☐ Female   ☐ Single

DATE OF BIRTH _____ / _____ / _____   AGE _____
               Mo.   Day   Yr.

NATIVE COUNTRY _____ LANGUAGE _____

NAME OF EMPLOYER _____

SIGNATURE _____ DATE _____

_____

Reading Practice

Exchange your completed form with a classmate. Read your partner's form. Complete the sentences.

1. My classmate's first name is _____ .

2. His/Her native country is _____ .

3. He/She lives in _____ .

4. He/She works for _____ .

More Practice: Vocabulary

An abbreviation is the short form of a word. Match the abbreviation with the correct word.

_____ **1.** M.I.   **a.** month

_____ **2.** Soc. Sec. #   **b.** number

_____ **3.** no.   **c.** year

_____ **4.** mo.   **d.** apartment

_____ **5.** Tues.   **e.** United States

_____ **6.** U.S.   **f.** telephone

_____ **7.** yr.   **g.** Social Security number

_____ **8.** apt.   **h.** middle initial

_____ **9.** tel.   **i.** Tuesday

Do you know other abbreviations? For example, do you know abbreviations for days of the week? Months of the year? Any others? Share your ideas with your classmates. See how many abbreviations the class knows.

Cultural Exchange

1. Ms. Jones asks her students to call her Cathy. What do you call your ESL teacher? What did you call your teacher in your native country?

2. What do people call *you*? Is it hard for people to say your name?

Application: Listening Practice

Listen to the questions. Write your answers to the questions.

1. _____   5. _____

2. _____   6. _____

3. _____   7. _____

4. _____   8. _____

Application: Writing Practice

Write the information.

1. What is your address?

_____

_____

2. What is your employer's address?

_____

_____

LESSON 3
Classmates & Co-Workers

Maria's Story

Who are your co-workers? Do you know them?
Do you talk to them? Are your co-workers from different
countries? Do they speak different languages?

🎧 Words for Work

cafeteria	kitchen	
co-workers	laundry	
department	linen	
housekeeping	maintenance	

🎧 More Words

nationality	fix
patient	hall
supervisor	meal
	tray

It is Tuesday. Today is our fourth ESL class. All of the students in my class work at Memorial Hospital with me. We are classmates and co-workers, but we don't know each other. We come from different countries. We are different nationalities.

Four of my co-workers in the kitchen are in my ESL class. Dung and Hoa are Vietnamese. They come from Vietnam. Dung, Hoa, and I get the meals ready. Hong is from China. Her nationality is Chinese. Hong puts the meals on the trays. Win is Cambodian. He washes the dishes.

Two classmates work in the housekeeping department. Sergio is Brazilian. He washes the floor in the cafeteria. He also cleans the patients' rooms. Luz comes from Puerto Rico. She cleans the bathrooms and the halls. Three of my classmates come from Haiti. Their names are Pierre, Isabelle, and Claire. Pierre works in maintenance. He fixes things at the hospital. Isabelle and Claire work in the laundry. There are a lot of sheets and towels at the hospital!

I see my classmates at work. We speak different languages, so we don't talk much. I want to talk to my classmates. I also want to talk to my supervisor and other people at the hospital.

Comprehension

Circle *yes* or *no* after each sentence.

1. The classmates come from many different countries.   yes   no

2. All of the classmates work in the same department.   yes   no

3. Maria works in the laundry.   yes   no

4. A kitchen worker puts the meals on the trays.   yes   no

5. Housekeeping workers wash the floors and clean the bathrooms.   yes   no

6. The hospital workers talk to each other a lot.   yes   no

Vocabulary

A. Complete each sentence with one of these words.

departments	kitchen	maintenance	supervisor
housekeeping	laundry	nationality	

1. Dung comes from Vietnam. His _____ is Vietnamese.

2. My _____ is my boss.

3. Maintenance and housekeeping are _____ at the hospital.

4. Workers in _____ fix things inside and outside the building.

5. Workers in _____ clean the bathrooms.

6. Workers in the _____ wash the linens.

7. Workers in the _____ cook meals.

B. Match each word with the correct meaning.

_____ 1. co-workers   **a.** breakfast, lunch, or dinner

_____ 2. cafeteria   **b.** repair

_____ 3. different   **c.** sick people in a hospital

_____ 4. meal   **d.** sheets, towels, pillowcases, tablecloths

_____ 5. tray   **e.** people you work with

_____ 6. fix   **f.** not the same

_____ 7. linens   **g.** something to carry food and dishes

_____ 8. patients   **h.** a place where you eat

Language Skills

Present Tense			
I	work	we	work
you	work	you	work
he } she } it }	works	they	work

A. Complete each sentence with the correct verb form.

Example: She <u>works</u> in a hospital.

1. (want) I _____ to learn English.

2. (know) Maria _____ her co-workers.

3. (like) They _____ their supervisor.

Present Tense Negative							
Full Form		**Contraction**		**Full Form**		**Contraction**	
I	do not	(don't) work		we	do not	(don't) work	
you	do not	(don't) work		you	do not	(don't) work	
he } she } it }	does not	(doesn't) work		they	do not	(don't) work	

B. Complete each sentence in the negative. Use the correct contraction.

Example: They <u>don't</u> go to ESL class on Sunday.

1. Maria _____ speak much English.

2. We _____ come from the same countries.

3. I _____ talk to my co-workers.

4. My supervisor _____ understand me.

🎧 Oral Practice: Pronunciation

A. Practice these words that begin with the letter _h_.

half	hard	help	hospital
hall	have	her	housekeeping
happy	he	his	how

Do you know other words that begin with the letter _h_?

B. Practice these sentences. Then say them as fast as you can.

1. Hana has Henry's hard hat.

2. He hung his hammer on the hook in the hall.

Oral Practice: Presentation

Fill in the following chart. Then tell your classmates about the place where you work.

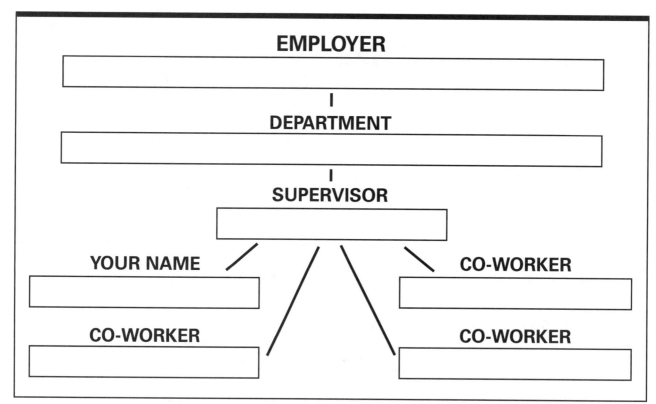

Reading Practice

A. Read the following story about Maria's classmate.

Hong is a Chinese woman in my ESL class. In class we talk about our families. Hong's mother and father live on a farm in China. They grow rice. My mother and father live on a farm in Mexico. They grow rice, too. Hong makes the same rice cakes my mother makes. I can't believe it! Hong is from China. I am from Mexico. But we eat the same food.

I see Hong in the cafeteria every day. She sits with other Chinese people. They speak Chinese. I eat lunch with my Mexican friends. We speak Spanish. I want to talk to Hong. I want to know more about China and Chinese food. Maybe we eat other food that is the same.

It's hard to talk to Hong. I don't think she can understand me. Sometimes I cannot understand her. I hope someday we can talk to each other.

B. Circle the letter of the correct answer.

1. Hong is _____.
   a. Mexican
   b. Chinese
   c. Cambodian

2. Maria and Hong both eat _____.
   a. corn
   b. rice
   c. beans

3. Every day Maria sees Hong _____.
   a. in the laundry
   b. on a farm
   c. in the cafeteria

4. Maria wants to know more about _____.
   a. Chinese food
   b. Mexican food
   c. American food

More Practice: Vocabulary

Match the country with the corresponding nationality.

_____ 1. Colombia   **a.** Cuban

_____ 2. Russia   **b.** Portuguese

_____ 3. Poland   **c.** Indian

_____ 4. India   **d.** Lebanese

_____ 5. Dominican Republic **e.** Colombian

_____ 6. Portugal   **f.** Algerian

_____ 7. Lebanon   **g.** Vietnamese

_____ 8. China   **h.** Russian

_____ 9. Cuba   **i.** Haitian

_____ 10. Algeria   **j.** Chinese

_____ 11. Haiti   **k.** Polish

_____ 12. Vietnam   **l.** Dominican

What is your nationality? What are the nationalities of your co-workers and classmates?

Cultural Exchange

1. Are there people in your ESL class from other countries? What countries are they from? Look at a map. Where are these countries? What do you know about these countries? What things are the same as in your country? What things are different? Food? Weather? Jobs? Families? Holidays? Sports? Schools? Discuss these things with your classmates.

2. Share something from your native country with your class (for example, a book, pictures, clothes, jewelry, or crafts).

Application

1. Do you work with people from other countries? From the U.S.? Do you talk to them? Why or why not?

2. Use the questions to interview a co-worker. Then tell your class about your co-worker. Complete the sentences to help you remember the information.

   a. What is your name?

   My co-worker's name is _____ .

   b. What country are you from?

   He/She is from _____ .

   c. What is the weather like in your country?

   The weather is _____ .

   d. What food do you like to eat?

   He/She likes to eat _____ .

   e. How many people are in your family?

   There are _____ people in his/her family.

   f. What was your job in your native country?

   He/She was a _____ .

   g. What is your job now?

   He/She is a _____ .

LESSON 4
Maria's Job

Maria's Story

What is your job?
Do you know all these jobs?

🎧 Words for Work

aide	gloves	punch in/out	
cart	hair net	supply room	
diet/dietary	measure/measurement	time card	
food-service worker	menu	uniform	

🎧 More Words

mix

peel

sharp

special

I work in the kitchen at the hospital. I'm a food-service worker. Every day I get to work at 7:00 A.M. First I punch in my time card. Then I go to the supply room. There I get a clean uniform and a hair net. Next I wash my hands with soap. After that I put on gloves. Then I get the food ready.

Some days I make fruit salad for lunch. I peel and cut up fruit. I cut up bananas, apples, peaches, and oranges. I mix all the fruit together. Every afternoon I get the vegetables ready for dinner. I cut potatoes, carrots, beans, and squash. I use a sharp knife, a clean cutting board, a large bowl, and a spoon. Then I help other workers put the meal trays on the cart.

I like working in the kitchen at the hospital. But I do the same thing almost every day. I want to get a different job. Maybe I can be a dietary aide. Dietary aides bring the menus to the patients. Maybe I can be a cook. I need to find out more about these jobs. I have a lot of questions. How much English do I need? Do I have to know about special diets? What do I have to learn?

Now I'm learning about food in my ESL class. I need to learn the measurements. I need to study the vocabulary. It's important to learn English. I want to get a new job soon.

Comprehension

Circle *yes* or *no* after each sentence.

1. Maria is a dishwasher.   yes   no

2. She punches in her time card every day.   yes   no

3. Some days Maria makes fruit salad.   yes   no

4. She uses sheets and towels to do her job.   yes   no

5. Maria does not like working in the hospital.   yes   no

6. Maria wants a new job.   yes   no

Vocabulary

A. Complete each sentence with one of these words.

cart	gloves	menu	time card
diet	hair nets	supply room	uniform

1. Many workers punch a _____ at the beginning and end of each day.

2. Maria goes to the _____ to get things for her job.

3. Some workers wear _____ on their hands.

4. Some workers wear _____ on their heads.

5. Oscar is too heavy. The doctor puts him on a _____ .

6. At the hospital, workers put the meal trays on a _____ .

7. A nurse at a hospital wears a _____ .

8. Patients look at a _____ to choose their food.

B. Circle the word that does not belong.

Example: breakfast   lunch   (salad)   dinner

1. knife   spoon   diet   bowl

2. cart   mix   cut   peel

3. fruit   vegetables   meat   menu

4. uniform   hair net   measurement   gloves

5. food-service worker   cook   housekeeper   dietary aide

6. learn   wash   study   read

Language Skills

Present Tense Questions					
Do	I	work?	Do	we	work?
Do	you	work?	Do	you	work?
Does	he she it	work?	Do	they	work?

A. Complete each question with the correct verb form.

Example: <u>Does</u> she <u>wear</u> gloves?

1. (like) _____ you _____ your job?

2. (cook) _____ they _____ the meals?

3. (work) _____ your supervisor _____ very hard?

4. (wash) _____ he _____ his hands?

5. (need) _____ I _____ a uniform?

6. (have) _____ the patients _____ fruit salad?

7. (know) _____ Maria _____ U.S. measurements?

B. Answer the questions with information about your job. Use the short-answer form.

Examples: Do you have two breaks every day?   <u>Yes, I do.</u> or <u>No, I don't.</u>

1. Do you wear a uniform at work?   _____

2. Do your co-workers come to work every day?   _____

3. Does your supervisor help you?   _____

4. Do you eat lunch in the cafeteria?   _____

5. Do you have a lot of work to do today?   _____

More Practice: Measurement

Weights and Measures

3 teaspoons (tsp.) = 1 tablespoon (tbsp.)	16 ounces (oz.) = 1 pound (lb.)
16 tbsp. = 1 cup (c.)	12 inches (in.) = 1 foot (ft.)
2 c. = 1 pint (pt.)	3 ft. = 1 yard (yd.)
2 pt. = 1 quart (qt.)	12 = 1 dozen (doz.)
4 qt. = 1 gallon (gal.)	

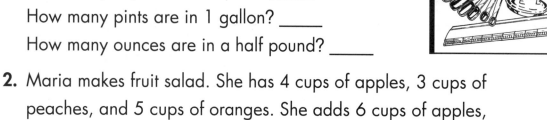

Read the problems. Then answer the questions.

1. How many cups are in 1 quart? _____
   How many pints are in 1 gallon? _____
   How many ounces are in a half pound? _____

2. Maria makes fruit salad. She has 4 cups of apples, 3 cups of peaches, and 5 cups of oranges. She adds 6 cups of apples, 9 cups of peaches, and 10 cups of oranges. How many cups of apples does she have? _____ How many cups of peaches? _____ How many cups of oranges? _____ How many cups of fruit salad does she make? _____

3. Hoshi uses milk to make pudding. She needs 4 cups. How many pints does she need? _____ How many quarts? _____

4. Thelma wants to make a birthday cake. She needs 4 tablespoons of sugar. She only has a teaspoon. How many teaspoons of sugar does Thelma need? _____

5. Hasan wants to buy 2 gallons of milk. The store doesn't have gallons. The store only has quarts. How many quarts does Hasan have to buy? _____

6. Luis is making his kitchen bigger. He wants to make it 10 feet wider. How many yards wider does he need to make it? _____

7. Al's Restaurant has two refrigerators. Each refrigerator is 27 inches wide. What is the total width in feet? _____

🎧 Listening Practice

Listen to the measurements. Write what you hear. Use numerals and abbreviations.

1. _____   5. _____

2. _____   6. _____

3. _____   7. _____

4. _____   8. _____

Discussion

1. Do you measure anything at work? What do you measure?
2. What do you use to measure things?

Cultural Exchange

1. What measurements do you use in your country?
2. Do you understand U.S. measurements?
3. Bring a recipe or food from your native country and share it with your class.

Application

Do you need to read in English at work? What do you read? What other ways do you need to use English at work? Use the form to help answer this question.

ENGLISH AT WORK

Why do you need English at work?

Circle *Yes* for things that are important. Circle *No* for things that are not important.

Speaking/Understanding

Who?			Where and When?		
Boss/Supervisor	Yes	No	Meetings	Yes	No
Co-workers	Yes	No	Problem	Yes	No
Personnel	Yes	No	Emergency	Yes	No
Customers	Yes	No	Telephone	Yes	No
Cafeteria Workers	Yes	No			
Other _____			Other _____		

Reading

What?			Where?		
Forms	Yes	No	Computer	Yes	No
Signs	Yes	No	Equipment	Yes	No
Notices	Yes	No	Materials	Yes	No
Directions	Yes	No	Newsletter	Yes	No
Orders	Yes	No	Bulletin Board	Yes	No
Other _____			Other _____		

Writing

What?			Who?		
Forms	Yes	No	Boss/Supervisor	Yes	No
Notes/Messages	Yes	No	Other Workers	Yes	No
Reports	Yes	No	Personnel	Yes	No
Orders	Yes	No	Customers	Yes	No
Other _____			Other _____		

Share the information on your form with your class.

UNIT 2
Ana's Story

Job Procedures and Benefits

LESSON 5
A Busy Schedule
Ana's Story

Work Schedule

	SUN.	MON.	TUES.	WED.	THURS.	FRI.	SAT.
Ana	Day off	8–4	8–4	8–4	8–4	8–4	OT 8–1
Felipe	12–8	10–6	10–6	Day off	Day off	7–3	8–4
Hana	8–4	8–4	7–3	10–6	8–4	OT 2-8	Day off
Rami	Day off	7–3	8–4	8–4	8–4	8–4	Day off
Marina	7–3	Day off	Day off	7–3	12–8	10–6	10–6
Ken	Day off	10–6	10–6	OT 2–8	9–5	9–5	9–5
Andre	7–3	7–3	Day off	OT 2–8	11–7	11–7	11–7
Rose	Day off	9–5	9–5	9–5	9–5	9–5	Day off

Do you have a schedule at work?
Do you have the same schedule every day?
Do you have the same schedule every week?

🎧 Words for Work

benefits	hotel	regular hours
break	on time	restaurant
full-time	overtime	schedule
health insurance	part-time	shift

🎧 More Words

bills
busy
cheap/expensive
medicine/medical

My name is Ana Rivera. I am Maria Garcia's sister. I work in a big hotel. My schedule is very busy. I work full-time. My regular hours are 8:00 A.M. to 4:00 P.M., Monday through Friday. Every morning I get up at 5:00. I get ready for work. I leave for the bus at 7:00. The hotel is far from my apartment. It takes a long time to get to work. I can't be late. My boss gets mad, and I lose pay. Most days I get to the hotel about 7:45. My first break is at 9:00. Lunch is at noon. I have another break at 2:00. I'm happy to have a second break. My feet are tired.

At 4:00 I finish work. I try to get home quickly. My husband, Ramón, works the second shift, from 3:00 to 11:00. He leaves the apartment at 2:30. He has to be on time for work. My son has a part-time job in a restaurant after school. My daughter comes home from school at 3:15. She is alone until I get home. I don't like to be late.

Ramón and I are very busy. But we need these jobs. We need the medical benefits, too. Health insurance is very important. Doctors and dentists cost a lot of money. Medicine is also expensive.

Some weekends Ramón and I work overtime. It's a busy schedule, but we need the money. We have a lot of bills. Nothing in the U.S. is cheap.

Comprehension

Circle *yes* or *no* after each sentence.

1. Ana has a full-time job.   yes   no

2. Her regular hours are 3 to 11.   yes   no

3. Ana has one break every day.   yes   no

4. Ramón works the second shift.   yes   no

5. Ana and Ramón work overtime every weekend.   yes   no

Vocabulary

Fill in the crossword puzzle with the correct words.

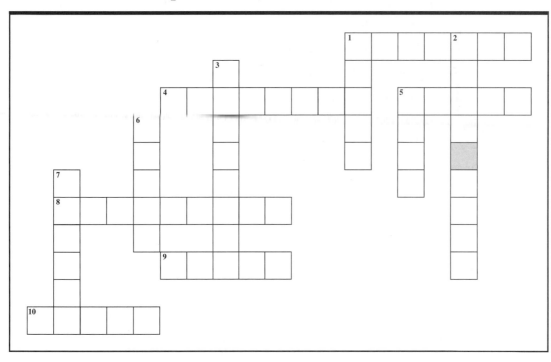

benefit
bills
break
busy
cheap
expensive
full-time
health
hotel
medicine
overtime
shift

Across

1. Health insurance is a _____.
4. You work more than 40 hours a week. You work _____.
5. You pay your _____ every month.
8. Something that costs a lot of money is _____.
9. Something that does not cost a lot of money is _____.
10. You work the first, second, or third _____.

Down

1. You stop working for a short time. You take a _____.
2. A _____ job is 40 hours a week.
3. The doctor sometimes gives you _____ to make you feel better.
5. You have a lot to do. You are _____.
6. Ana works in a big, beautiful _____.
7. Your _____ insurance helps to pay the doctor and hospital bills.

Language Skills

A. Complete each question Then answer each question with the short-answer form.

Example: (speak) <u>Can</u> you <u>speak</u> English?   <u>Yes, I can.</u> *or* <u>No, I can't.</u>

1. (help) _____ you _____ me?   _____

2. (have) _____ I _____ more overtime?   _____

3. (work) _____ you _____ for me on Saturday?   _____

4. (go) _____ we _____ to lunch at 1:00 today?   _____

5. (leave) _____ I _____ early this week?   _____

B. With a partner, make as many questions as you can. Use the words in the box. Ask each other the questions and answer them.

Example: <u>Can you go home in September?</u> <u>Yes, I can.</u> *or* <u>No, I can't.</u>

Can you	work eat lunch take a break work overtime	on January 10? at 11:30? tomorrow night? on Thursday? in the afternoon? from 9 to 5?

⌒ Oral Practice: Dialogue

Practice asking for time off. Use your supervisor's name for the first blank below. Use the words and sentences in numbers 1–5 to complete the dialogue. For number 6, write your own ideas. Practice with a partner.

EMPLOYEE: Excuse me, _____*(name of supervisor)*_____ , can I talk to you?
SUPERVISOR: Sure.

EMPLOYEE: Can I have _____*(a)*_____ off? _____*(b)*_____ .
SUPERVISOR: OK.

1. a. Friday morning
   b. I have to talk to my child's teacher.

2. a. next Monday afternoon
   b. I have to go to Immigration.

3. a. next Thursday morning
   b. I have to go to the doctor at 10:00.

4. a. tomorrow night
   b. I have a personal problem.

5. a. Wednesday, February 24
   b. I have to go to court.

6. a. _____

   b. _____

⌒ Listening Practice

Listen to the times, days, and dates. Write what you hear.

1. _____   5. _____   9. _____

2. _____   6. _____   10. _____

3. _____   7. _____   11. _____

4. _____   8. _____   12. _____

Reading Practice

Read the following time card. Then answer the questions.

Employee Name **Tam Nguyen**   Employee No. **6524**

Time Beginning: **11/13/03**   Time Ending: **11/18/03**   Shift: **first**

DAY	IN	OUT	IN	OUT	TOTAL
Monday	8:00	11:30	12:00	4:30	
Tuesday	7:30	11:00	11:30	4:00	
Wednesday	7:30	11:00	11:30	4:30	
Thursday	8:00	11:30	12:00	5:30	
Friday	7:30	11:00	11:30	4:30	
Saturday	8:00	12:00			
				Total Hours	

Signature: *Tam Nguyen*   Approved by: *Bob Davis*

1. What shift did Tam work?

2. How much time does Tam take for lunch each day?

3. How many hours did Tam work each day? Write the totals on the form.

4. How many hours did Tam work this week? Write the total hours on the form.

5. Tam gets overtime when he works more than 8 hours in one day. He also gets overtime when he works on Saturday. How many overtime hours did Tam work?

🎧 More Practice: Reading

A. Read the following story about Susana.

My name is Susana. I come from Brazil. I came to the U.S. nine months ago. In Brazil, sometimes people are late. No one gets upset.

The U.S. is different. It's very busy here. Everyone is in a hurry. People talk fast. People move fast. It's important to be on time.

In the U.S. it isn't good to be late for work. My boss always watches the clock. I can't be late. My boss gets mad. We have a very busy schedule at work. But today my bus was late. Now I'm late for work. I hope my boss isn't mad.

B. Circle the letter of the correct answer.

1. Susana came to the U.S. _____ .
   a. nine weeks ago
   b. nine months ago
   c. nine years ago

2. Where Susana comes from, people _____ .
   a. move fast
   b. like to wait
   c. are sometimes late

3. Susana has a _____ at work.
   a. good boss
   b. lot of friends
   c. busy schedule

4. Today Susana is _____ .
   a. on time
   b. mad at her boss
   c. late for work

5. In the U.S. it's important to be _____ .
   a. in a hurry
   b. on time
   c. busy

Cultural Exchange

1. Is it important to be on time in your native country? Explain.
2. Was being on time hard when you came to the U.S.? Explain.

Let's Think about It

Look at each reason for being late for work. Is it a good reason?
Circle *yes* or *no*.

1. The weather is bad.   yes   no
2. You have to go to the airport.   yes   no
3. Your child is sick.   yes   no
4. Your car won't start.   yes   no
5. There is a lot of traffic.   yes   no
6. You get up late. You miss the bus.   yes   no
7. You have an emergency at home.   yes   no
8. You are tired.   yes   no

Application

1. What do you say to your boss when you are late? Discuss with your class. Write a dialogue with a partner. Present it.
2. Keep your schedule at work for a week. Write what you do each day. Bring your schedule to class. Tell the class about it.

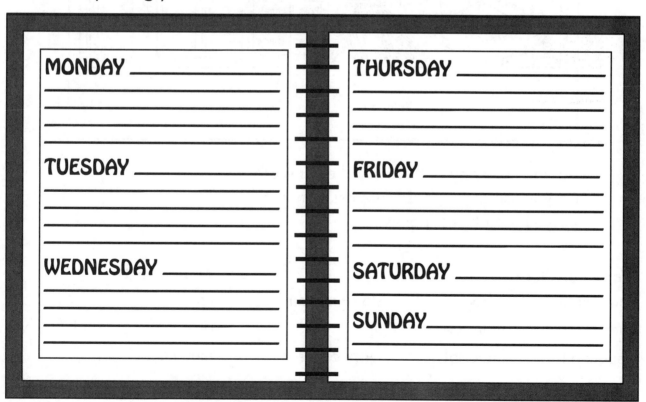

MONDAY _____
TUESDAY _____
WEDNESDAY _____
THURSDAY _____
FRIDAY _____
SATURDAY _____
SUNDAY _____

LESSON 6
Ana's New Job

Ana's Story

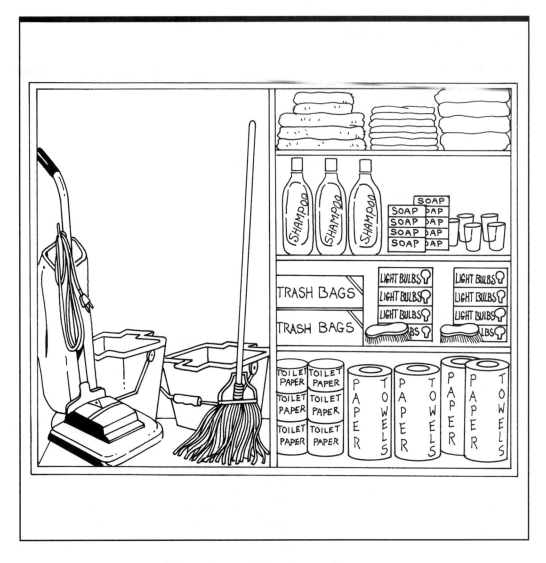

Do you have any of these supplies at work?
Do you use any of these supplies at home?
Do you use other supplies?

🎧 **Words for Work**

equipment	lobby	storage room
guest	manager	tip
inspection	materials	work order

🎧 **More Words**

check	in order
dust	shelf/shelves
elevator	

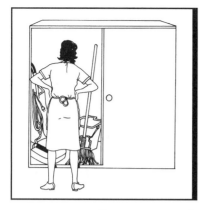

I got my job at the hotel two months ago. It's a good place to work. I work in the housekeeping department. I'm a housekeeper. I clean the guest rooms, the halls, and the lobby.

I get to work every morning about 7:45. First I get my work order. Next I go to the storage room and get my cart. Then I get the supplies I need.

The supplies are on shelves in the storage room. Everything is in order. The paper towels are on the bottom shelf, next to the toilet paper. Trash bags are on the second shelf, next to the light bulbs. The soap is on the third shelf, between the glasses and the shampoo. There are pails on the floor, behind the vacuum and the mop.

The linens are on the top shelf. There are towels, pillowcases, and sheets. The pillowcases are between the towels and the sheets.

Today the manager is here for an inspection. First she checks my equipment and materials. Then we take the elevator to the third floor. We go to Room 363. The manager watches me work. First I clean the bathroom. I use a mop, cleaners, brush, and paper towels. I put clean towels on a shelf above the toilet. I put other supplies on a shelf above the sink. Then I clean the bedroom. I use a dust cloth and vacuum cleaner. I get the clean sheets and make the beds. The manager checks all of my work. This makes me very nervous. I ask her, "Is everything OK?" She says, "You're doing a good job."

It isn't easy to be a housekeeper. The work is hard, and I don't make much money. But sometimes I get a big tip. I like that! Also, I'm learning new things and meeting new people. My co-workers are nice. We talk at break and at lunch. Sometimes I talk to the guests, too. My English is a little better now. I think this job is good for me.

Comprehension

A. Circle *yes* **or** *no* **after each sentence.**

1. Ana works in the housekeeping department.   yes   no

2. The cleaning supplies are on shelves in the storage room.   yes   no

3. They aren't easy to find.   yes   no

4. Ana cleans the bathrooms with a vacuum cleaner and a
   dust cloth.   yes   no

5. Ana isn't doing a good job.   yes   no

6. Sometimes Ana gets a tip.   yes   no

B. Circle the letter of the correct answer.

1. Ana's job is _____ .
   a. in a restaurant
   b. in a hospital
   c. in a hotel

2. Ana gets her work order and supplies. Then she goes _____ .
   a. home
   b. to lunch
   c. to work

3. Ana's _____ checks her work.
   a. manager
   b. friend
   c. co-worker

4. Ana thinks her job is good because _____ .
   a. she makes a lot of money
   b. she is learning new things
   c. she works hard

Vocabulary

A. Complete each sentence with one of these words.

elevator	guest	storage room
equipment	inspection	work order

1. The supplies are kept in the _____ .

2. A person who stays in a hotel is a _____ .

3. Some workers use _____ to do their jobs.

4. Ana knows what to do each day. She gets a _____ .

5. Your boss checks your work. This is an _____ .

6. You take an _____ to go from the first floor to the tenth floor.

B. Circle the word that does not belong.

Example: bedroom   bathroom   (hotel)   kitchen

1. shelf   brush   paper towels   dust cloth

2. soap   shampoo   glasses   bathroom

3. towels   guest   linen   sheets

4. equipment   supplies   inspection   materials

5. lobby   guest room   storage room   bed

6. behind   next to   tip   above

Language Skills

A. **Look at the supply closet. Then complete the sentences with one of the following prepositions.**

above	behind	below	between	next to

Example: The light bulbs are <u>below</u> the glasses.

1. The soap is _____ the glasses and the shampoo.

2. The vacuum is _____ the mop.

3. The sheets are _____ the glasses.

4. The paper towels are _____ the light bulbs.

5. The pails are _____ the vacuum and the mop.

B. Look at the supply closet on page 50. Work with a partner. Ask and answer questions about where the supplies are stored.

Example: <u>Where is the shampoo?</u> <u>On the shelf next to the soap.</u>

🎧 Listening Practice: Pronunciation

A. Listen to the words that end in *es*. How many parts do you hear? Write the number.

Example: watches   2

1. glasses ____	**7.** gloves ____	**13.** boxes ____
2. knives ____	**8.** peaches ____	**14.** shelves ____
3. mixes ____	**9.** sponges ____	**15.** brushes ____
4. services ____	**10.** aides ____	**16.** languages ____
5. oranges ____	**11.** dishes ____	**17.** lunches ____
6. washes ____	**12.** fixes ____	**18.** telephones ____

B. Practice saying the words.

C. Practice the following sentences. Then say them as fast as you can.

1. Alexis fixes the lunches and puts them in boxes.
2. The aides put the gloves and the knives on the shelves.
3. She washes the dishes with brushes and sponges.

🎧 Listening Practice: Following Directions

Part 1. Listen to the dialogues. Say the answers to the questions you hear.

Part 2. Listen to the directions. Then see if you can repeat them in the same order.

Writing Practice

A. Write about Ana's job. Use information from the story on page 47.

Ana works in the _____ department. She is

1

a (job) _____. She does many things every day.

2

First she _____.

3

Then she _____.

4

Next she _____.

5

Ana uses a _____, a _____,

6   7

and a _____ to do her job.

8

B. Now write about your job.

I work in the _____ department. I am a/an

(job) _____. I do many things in my job.

First I _____.

Then I _____.

Next I _____.

I use a/an _____ , a/an _____ ,

and a/an _____ to do my job.

More Practice: Vocabulary

Ana uses a mop, cleaners, and other supplies to do her job.
What supplies, equipment, and materials do you have at work?
Write these words in the box.

a _pron_ _____ i _____ r _____

b _____ j _____ s _____

c _____ k _____ t _____

d _____ l _____ u _____

e _____ m _____ v _____

f _____ n _____ w _____

g _____ o _____ y _____

h _____ p _____ z _____

Application

1. Is there a storage room or closet where you work? What is in it?

2. Tell the class about your job. Use what you wrote on page 52.

LESSON 7
Time Off

Ana's Story

Do you ever take time off?
When do you take time off?
Why do you take time off?

🎧 Words for Work

call in sick	personal day
cover for	sick day/time
day off/time off	unpaid/paid
holiday	vacation

🎧 More Words

ache	message
appointment	office
fever	problem
flu	sore throat

Today I am sick. I have a headache and a sore throat. My whole body aches. I think I also have a fever. I feel terrible! One of my co-workers has the flu. Maybe I have the flu.

I can't go to work today. I am too sick. I have to call the doctor's office. I need to make an appointment. Maybe the doctor can give me some medicine. I also have to call my boss, Ms. Richards. This morning I leave a message. I say, "This is Ana Rivera. I cannot come to work today. I'm very sick. I have to go to the doctor. I'll call you tomorrow."

It's important to call in sick. Ms. Richards has to find someone to cover for me. This can be a problem. It's hard to change the schedule. I hope we're not very busy today. I don't want Ms. Richards to be mad at me.

I have one more problem. I started working at the hotel two months ago. I get five paid holidays, one personal day, two weeks' vacation, and five sick days at this job. But I am a new worker. So I don't get any sick days yet. I have to take the day off without pay. I don't want to take unpaid time off.

I can't be out of work very long. I hope the doctor can help me. Maybe he can give me some medicine. I have to get better fast. I want to get back to work.

Comprehension

A. Circle *yes* or *no*.

1. Ana has a sore throat and a fever.   yes   no

2. She has a doctor's appointment at 9:00.   yes   no

3. It's important to call in sick.   yes   no

4. It's easy to change the schedule.   yes   no

5. Ana can take five sick days now.   yes   no

6. Ana doesn't want to get back to work.   yes   no

B. Circle the letter of the correct answer.

1. Ana feels _____ today.
   a. good
   b. terrible
   c. tired

2. She cannot _____.
   a. go to work
   b. talk on the telephone
   c. take medicine

3. Ana has to call _____.
   a. her husband
   b. her co-worker
   c. her boss and her doctor

4. Ana has to take _____.
   a. a holiday
   b. a vacation day
   c. unpaid time off

Vocabulary

A. Complete each sentence with one of these words or phrases.

appointment	cover for	unpaid
calls in sick	holidays	vacation

1. Labor Day and Memorial Day are _____ for workers in the U.S.

2. You make an _____ to see a doctor.

3. In her new job Pilar has five sick days and two weeks' _____ .

4. Fatima has the flu. She can't go to work. She _____ .

5. I am sick. My co-worker has to _____ me.

6. A worker takes time off and doesn't get paid. This is _____ time.

B. Circle the word that does not belong.

Example: hospital   nurse   (schedule)   doctor

1. sore throat   headache   problem   backache

2. office   holiday   sick day   personal day

3. doctor   appointment   medicine   vacation

4. fever   message   cold   flu

Language Skills

Present Tense of *Have*			
I	have	we	have
you	have	you	have
he she it }	has	they	have

A. Complete each sentence with the correct verb form.

Example: He <u>has</u> good benefits.

1. I _____ a headache.

2. Pavit _____ a backache today.

3. We _____ an inspection every year.

4. She _____ a new manager.

5. They _____ different schedules.

Questions with *Have*					
Do	I	have	Do	we	have
Do	you	have	Do	you	have
Does {	he she it	have	Do	they	have

B. Complete each question.

Example: <u>Do</u> you <u>have</u> the bleach?

1. ____ Fernando and Paul _____ the same supervisor?

2. ____ you _____ a knife?

3. ____ we _____ a big work order today?

4. ____ Han _____ a cold?

5. ____ Parvin _____ a uniform?

🎧 Oral Practice: Pronunciation

A. Practice the letter *p*.

paid	people
paper	print
part-time	problem
patient	punch in

Practice the letter *f*.

family	flu
feel	form
fifth	friend
five	full-time

Do you know other words with the letters *p* and *f* ?

B. Practice these sentences. Then say them as fast as you can.

1. Franco fills out the first form for his friend.
2. The patients have problems and hope to get help.
3. Four part-time people get paid every Friday.

🎧 Oral Practice: Dialogue

Practice calling in sick. Use your name for the first blank below. Use the words and sentences in numbers 1–5 to complete the dialogue. For number 6, write your own ideas. Practice with a partner.

EMPLOYEE: This is _____(your name)_____ . I cannot come to work today.
SUPERVISOR: What's the problem?

EMPLOYEE: _____a._____ .
SUPERVISOR: That's too bad. When can you come back to work?

EMPLOYEE: _____b._____ .
SUPERVISOR: Please call me tomorrow.

EMPLOYEE: OK.

1. **a.** I'm sick. I have a bad cold.
   b. In a couple of days.

2. **a.** I have an emergency at home.
   b. Tomorrow, I think.

3. **a.** I hurt my back.
   b. I don't know.

4. **a.** I have the flu.
   b. In a few days.

5. **a.** My child is sick.
   b. On Friday.

6. **a.** _____
   b. _____

Reading Practice

Ana called in sick. She left a message for her boss with
a co-worker. Read her message.

Date __2/25/03__

Time __8:10__   (AM)   PM

To __Ms. Richards__

From __Sun Park__

Message __Ana Rivera can't come to work today. She is sick.__

__She will call tomorrow.__

Answer the following questions.

1. What is the date of the message? _____

2. What time is it? Is it morning or night? _____

3. Why can't Ana go to work? _____

⌒ Listening Practice

A. Listen to the message. Write what you hear.

Date _____

Time _____   AM   PM

To _____

From _____

Message _____

_____

B. Now use this form to practice the messages you take at work. Work with a partner. Use your boss's name after *To*. Use your name after *From*. Write the message your partner says.

Date _____

Time _____   AM   PM

To _____

From _____

Message _____

_____

Let's Think about It

A. Ana has to take time off from work because she is sick. Look at each reason for taking time off. Is it a good reason? Circle *yes* or *no*.

1. Your car needs to be fixed.   yes   no
2. You have a headache.   yes   no
3. Your babysitter is sick.   yes   no
4. You have to go to a funeral.   yes   no
5. You have to get your driver's license. yes   no
6. You are moving.   yes   no
7. You are tired.   yes   no
8. It is your religious holiday.   yes   no

B. What are some other good reasons for taking time off? What are some bad reasons? Share your ideas with your classmates.

Cultural Exchange

1. What are common medicines in your native country? What do people in your country take or do for a cold? A cough? A fever? A headache? A stomachache?

2. There are a lot of different medicines in the U.S. What do you take when you are sick?

Application

1. Practice calling in sick. Use your boss's name for the first blank. Use your name for the second blank. You may need to spell your name. Give a reason for calling in sick. Work with a partner, and present your dialogue to the class. Check that your teacher and your classmates can understand you.

   Example: <u>Ms. Richards</u>, this is <u>Ana</u>. I can't come to work today. <u>I have a bad cold</u>.

   _____, this is _____. I can't come to work

   today. _____ .

2. Practice asking for time off. Use your boss's name for the first blank. Give a reason you may need to take time off. Work with a partner, and present your dialogue to the class. Check that your teacher and your classmates can understand you.

   Example: <u>Ms. Richards</u>, have you got a minute? I have a question. <u>Can I take my vacation next month</u>?

   _____ , have you got a minute? I have a question.

   _____ ?

LESSON 8
Getting Paid

Ana's Story

Employee Name			Employee #		Pay Period
Vinit Patel			46355		09/14/03 — 09/20/03

	Hours	Rate	Earnings	Year-to-Date	Deductions
Regular	40	$10.50	$420.00	$16,385	$30.00 Fed. Tax
Overtime	10	$15.75	$157.50	$3,150	$22.54 State Tax
					$42.58 FICA
					$60.00 Medical Ins.

TOTAL DEDUCTIONS ➡	$155.12
GROSS PAY ➡	$577.50
NET PAY ➡	$422.38

Do you get a paycheck?
Does your pay stub look like this one?
What are your deductions?

🎧 Words for Work

deduction	gross pay/net pay	take-home pay
earn/earnings	paycheck	time and a half
federal/state taxes	pay period	withholding
FICA	pay stub	year-to-date

🎧 More Words

add
government
subtract
total

I'm so happy it's Friday! I got paid this morning. The pay stub shows my earnings for this pay period. It also shows my earnings so far this year. Those are my year-to-date earnings. Deductions are on the pay stub, too. Some deductions are federal and state withholding taxes. The government takes money out of my pay.

I don't understand everything on my pay stub. Why is there a deduction for medical benefits? What is *FICA*? I ask my friend Rosa. She works with me at the hotel. Rosa explains that the hotel pays half of my health insurance. The other half comes out of my pay. Rosa also tells me that *FICA* is the deduction for Social Security.

Rosa explains gross pay and net pay. Gross pay is money I earn before deductions. I add my deductions and subtract them from my gross pay. This is my net pay. It is also called take-home pay. After deductions, my take-home pay looks small.

This week my paycheck is bigger. I'm working overtime every Saturday now. I have 6 hours of overtime. I get time and a half for overtime. This makes a big difference in my paycheck.

There's a lot of information on my pay stub. I check it every week. I tell my boss if there is a problem.

Comprehension

A. Circle *yes* or *no* after each sentence.

1. Ana gets paid every Thursday.   yes   no

2. Her pay stub shows earnings and deductions.   yes   no

3. Rosa is Ana's sister.   yes   no

4. Social Security is not a deduction.   yes   no

5. This week Ana's paycheck is bigger because she worked   yes   no
   overtime.

B. Circle the letter of the correct answer.

1. Rosa helps Ana understand _____ .
    a. her schedule
    b. her pay stub
    c. her bills

2. Ana pays _____ of her health insurance.
    a. all
    b. none
    c. half

3. Net pay is also called _____ .
    a. gross pay
    b. take-home pay
    c. FICA

4. Ana's paycheck is _____ after deductions.
    a. smaller
    b. bigger
    c. the same

Vocabulary

A. Complete each sentence with one of these words or phrases.

deduction	federal withholding tax	pay stub
earn	pay period	time and a half

1. A _____ shows earnings and deductions.

2. You get paid every week. Your _____ is one week.

3. You are paid _____ for overtime.

4. The money you make is the money you _____ .

5. FICA is the _____ for Social Security.

6. The _____ is for the U.S. government.

B. Match each word or phrase with the correct meaning.

_____ **1.** full-time   **a.** Social Security

_____ **2.** overtime   **b.** less than 40 hours a week

_____ **3.** net pay   **c.** earnings before deductions

_____ **4.** deduct   **d.** 40 hours a week

_____ **5.** gross pay   **e.** earnings so far this year

_____ **6.** FICA   **f.** more than 40 hours a week

_____ **7.** earnings year-to-date   **g.** subtract; take away

_____ **8.** part-time   **h.** earnings after deductions

Language Skills

Present Continuous Tense			
I	am working	we	are working
you	are working	you	are working
he			
she }	is working	they	are working
it			

A. Complete each sentence with the correct verb form.

Example: Ana <u>is working</u> overtime today.

1. (do) You _____ a good job.

2. (wash) They _____ the floors now.

3. (talk) Cho _____ to the doctor.

4. (work) We _____ at the hotel.

5. (help) I _____ my boss now.

Present Continuous Tense Questions

Am	I	working?	Are	we	working?
Are	you	working?	Are	you	working?
Is	he she it	working?	Are	they	working?

B. Complete each question with the correct verb form. Then answer each question. Use the short-answer form.

Example: (save) <u>Is</u> he <u>saving</u> to buy a car?   <u>Yes, he is.</u> *or* <u>No, he isn't.</u>

1. (eat) ____ your supervisor _____ lunch now?   _____ .

2. (take) ____ you _____ your break now?   _____ .

3. (cover) ____ your co-worker _____ for you this week?   _____ .

4. (study) ____ you _____ English?   _____ .

🎧 Oral Practice: Dialogue

Practice asking about your paycheck. Use your supervisor's name for the first blank. Use sentences 1–4 to complete the dialogue. Write your own ideas for number 5. Practice with a partner.

Example: EMPLOYEE: *(name of supervisor)* , I have a question about my paycheck.

SUPERVISOR: What's the problem?

EMPLOYEE: _____ .

SUPERVISOR: I'll check on it for you.

EMPLOYEE: Thanks a lot.

1. I think my hours are wrong.

2. I was out sick last Tuesday, and I didn't get my sick pay.

3. I don't understand. I have a bigger medical deduction this week.

4. I worked overtime on Thursday. I didn't get paid for it.

5. _____ .

Reading Practice

A. Read the following poem about a paycheck.

On my paycheck I can see
a deduction for Social Security,
taxes like federal and state,
and all my earnings year-to-date.

Health insurance is a benefit for me
and everyone in my family.
I work hard for my gross pay;
net is all I take away.

Forty hours is my regular week,
but overtime pay makes me speak
to my boss and ask him when
I can work more hours again!

B. Answer the questions. Fill in the answers on the pay stub below.

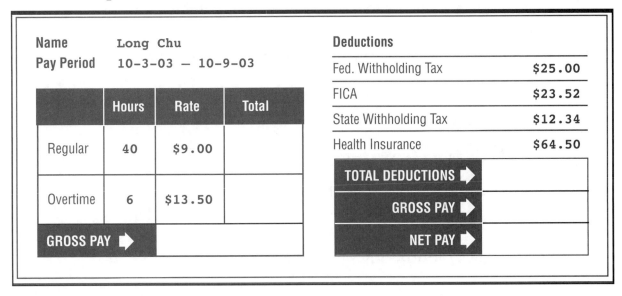

Name	Long Chu		
Pay Period	10-3-03 — 10-9-03		

	Hours	Rate	Total
Regular	40	$9.00	
Overtime	6	$13.50	
GROSS PAY ➡			

Deductions

Fed. Withholding Tax	$25.00
FICA	$23.52
State Withholding Tax	$12.34
Health Insurance	$64.50
TOTAL DEDUCTIONS ➡	
GROSS PAY ➡	
NET PAY ➡	

1. What is Long's pay period? What is your pay period?

2. How much did Long make in overtime?

3. What is Long's gross pay?

4. How much does Long pay in withholding taxes?

5. What are his total deductions?

6. What is Long's take-home pay?

🎧 More Practice: Reading

A. Read the story about Josef and Mario.

Friday is payday at Silva Construction Company. Most Fridays everyone is happy. Today was different. There was a fight.

Josef found Mario's pay stub. Josef showed the pay stub to the other guys. Mario got mad. Josef and Mario had a fight. The boss sent them home for three days. They lose three days' pay.

The boss said, "In the U.S. you don't show a pay stub to anyone. A pay stub is personal. And if you have a problem, you go to your boss. Don't fight. You can lose your job."

Josef and Mario were lucky this time. They didn't get fired. Today everyone learned something about working in the U.S.

B. Number the sentences from 1 to 6 to show the correct order.

_____ Josef and Mario go home.

_____ Mario gets mad.

_____ Josef finds Mario's pay stub.

_____ Josef and Mario have a fight.

_____ The boss talks to everyone.

_____ Josef shows Mario's pay stub to the other guys.

C. Answer the following questions. Discuss your answers with the class.

1. The boss sends Mario and Josef home. Is this fair? What do you think?

2. Mario and Josef lose three days' pay. Is this fair? What do you think?

3. Do people talk about their pay where you work?

4. Do people sometimes fight at work? What does the boss do?

Cultural Exchange

Do people fight at work in your native country? What happens?

Application

1. Look at your pay stub. What are the deductions? Make a list. Bring your list to class.

2. What are your benefits? Do you have these benefits?

   - Health insurance?   yes   no

   - Paid vacation?   yes   no

     How much time? _____

   - Paid holidays?   yes   no

     Which ones? _____

     _____

   - Sick days?   yes   no

     How many days? _____

   - Personal days?   yes   no

     How many? _____

3. Who do you talk to at work when you have a problem with your pay?

   _____

UNIT 3
Joe's Story

Job Safety

LESSON 9
Change Is Hard

Joe's Story

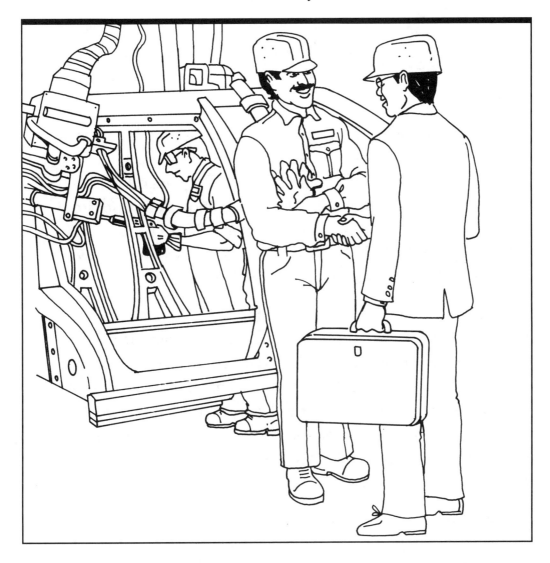

Are there changes where you work?
Are there new people? Are there new products? Are there new
machines? Are there any other changes?

 Words for Work

caution	flammable	product	teamwork
factory	hazardous	safety	warning
fire alarm	machine	team	
fire extinguisher	poison	team member	

More Words

change
comfortable
get used to
label

My name is José Garcia. People call me Joe. I am Maria's husband. I came to the U.S. three years ago. I got a job at a factory near my apartment. Many people from my country worked there. I was comfortable at this job. Now many things at the factory are changing.

There are a lot of new employees. They need to learn many things. New employees have to understand their work schedules, time cards, pay, and benefits. They need to know about safety. They have to find the fire extinguishers and fire alarms. They have to read signs like EMERGENCY EXIT, DANGER, and CAUTION. Most of these new workers know only a little English. They need a lot of help.

There are also new teams at the factory. Team members have to talk about work orders, materials, and products. We have to talk about problems. We have to help each other. We have to learn other jobs. We sometimes have to teach our jobs to co-workers. Teamwork is hard. It's even harder with all the new people. They come from different countries. They speak different languages. It isn't always easy for everyone to work together.

There are a lot of new products at the factory, too. Some of them are dangerous. Everyone needs to read the labels on these products. The labels have safety warnings on them. Words like *flammable*, *hazardous*, and *poison* are on the labels. There are many other important words we need to know.

There are also new machines at the factory. We have to learn about these new machines. There is a lot to understand.

Many things are changing at the factory. There are new people, new teams, new products, and new machines. It takes time to get used to all these new things. Change is hard!

Comprehension

**A. Circle the letter of the correct answer(s). There may be one or
two answers for each sentence.**

1. Joe came to the U.S. _____ .
   a. last week
   b. last year
   c. three years ago

2. Joe works _____ .
   a. near his apartment
   b. at a factory
   c. at a hotel

3. New employees need to _____ .
   a. work overtime
   b. read signs
   c. find the fire extinguishers

4. Employees work in teams. They
   have to _____ .
   a. talk about problems
   b. work alone
   c. help each other

5. The labels on products have _____
   on them.
   a. safety warnings
   b. work schedules
   c. important words

B. Answer the following questions.

1. What are the changes at the factory? There are new _____,

   new _____, new _____, and new

   _____ .

2. Joe says, "Change is hard." What does he mean?
   Is change hard for you?

   _____

Vocabulary

A. Complete each sentence with one of these words or phrases.

comfortable	labels	poison
fire alarm	machines	team member

1. Many workers in a factory use _____ to do their jobs.

2. You work with a group of people. You are a _____ .

3. The _____ on many products have safety warnings on them.

4. If there is a fire at work, you pull the _____ .

5. Drinking bleach can make you very sick. Bleach is a _____ .

6. You like your job, your boss, and your co-workers. You feel

   _____ at work.

B. Match each word or phrase with the correct meaning.

_____ 1. hazardous   **a.** things you make

_____ 2. team   **b.** something you use to put out a fire

_____ 3. flammable   **c.** a building where things are made

_____ 4. products   **d.** dangerous

_____ 5. caution   **e.** something new; not the same

_____ 6. factory   **f.** a group of people working together

_____ 7. change   **g.** warning; be careful

_____ 8. fire extinguisher   **h.** burns easily

Language Skills

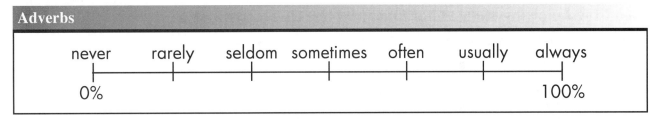

Adverbs

never   rarely   seldom   sometimes   often   usually   always

0%   100%

Complete each sentence with an adverb from the box above.
Write about yourself.

Example: I <u>often</u> eat lunch with my co-workers.

1. I _____ take a bus to work.

2. I _____ start work at 7:30 A.M.

3. I _____ come late to work.

4. I _____ work hard.

5. I _____ read labels.

6. I _____ understand my boss.

7. I _____ have a headache.

8. I _____ help my co-workers.

9. I _____ use a fire extinguisher.

10. I _____ work overtime.

11. I _____ get a break in the morning.

12. I _____ work in a team.

🎧 Reading Practice

Read the following story about Olga and her co-worker Lidia. Then answer the questions.

My name is Olga. I work in a nursing home. There is a new employee in my department. Her name is Lidia. Lidia comes from Russia, and she only speaks a little English.

Lidia is a nice person. She works hard and tries to do a good job. But sometimes Lidia makes mistakes. She doesn't always understand directions. She can't read all the signs and labels. Lidia doesn't like to ask our boss for help. She is afraid he will get mad.

Most of the time I can help Lidia. But sometimes I get very busy. Then I have to say, "Lidia, I can't help you now. You need to ask the boss. Don't be nervous. It's easy. You just say, 'I don't understand. Can you please help me?'"

Next week I will be on vacation, and Lidia will have to work alone. I hope she isn't afraid to ask for help. The boss is a nice guy. He doesn't get mad when people ask for help. But he does get mad when people make mistakes.

1. Where do Olga and Lidia work?

2. Why does Lidia make mistakes?

3. Does Lidia ask her boss for help? Why or why not?

4. What should Lidia say to her boss?

Discussion

1. Do you sometimes need help at work? Why?

2. Who do you ask for help? Your boss? A co-worker? A friend? Why? What do you say?

Application

There are many signs and labels at the factory where Joe Garcia works. These are some of the signs and labels. Some of the signs and labels are pictures.

1. Do you understand all these signs and labels?
2. Do you have the same signs and labels where you work?
3. Do you have other signs and labels where you work?
4. Make a list of all the signs and labels you have at work. Share your list with your class. Are there warning labels on the products you use at home? Bring them in or copy them. Share them with your class.

LESSON 10
Safety on the Job
Joe's Story

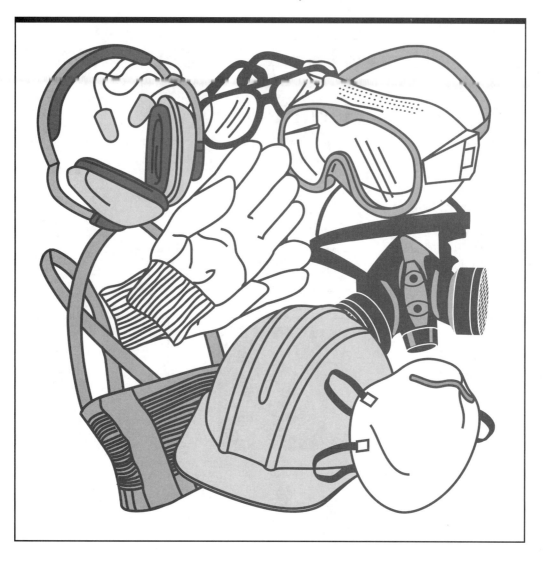

Do you wear safety gear at work?
What do you wear?
Why is safety gear important?

🎧 **Words for Work**

assembly	harmful	safety glasses
back-support belt	mask	safety rules
earmuffs/earplugs	respirator	training
fumes	safety gear	

🎧 **More Words**

building	wear
noisy	
parts	
required	

One of the new people at the factory is a guy from Guatemala. His name is Carlos. Carlos and his wife, Rosa, live in my neighborhood. Rosa works in the restaurant down the street. I got Carlos a job at the factory. He works with me in the assembly department. We make parts for cars and trucks.

This week Carlos is in training. Yesterday was his first day. I'm a team leader now. I had to tell Carlos about his job and about safety at the factory. First I told him about the safety rules. Every department has rules. The rules for the assembly department are on the wall near the supervisor's desk. Carlos has to know these rules. Some rules are about wearing safety gear. Other rules are about using machines and equipment. Everyone in the department has to follow the safety rules.

At 9:00 Carlos and I walked around the building. I showed Carlos the emergency exits, fire alarms, and fire extinguishers. It is important to know where they are. I also showed him the cafeteria and the bathrooms. Then we went to every department. I showed Carlos all of the safety gear. Safety gear is required at the factory. In the assembly department we wear gloves and safety glasses. In the shop the employees wear earmuffs. They use big machines there. These big machines are very noisy. They also use a lot of heavy equipment. Some employees wear a back-support belt. In the sanding area the workers wear masks. There is a lot of dust. Workers in the painting room wear respirators. The fumes from the paint can be harmful. People can get sick. It is important for everyone to wear their safety gear.

At 10:00 Carlos and I took a coffee break. After the coffee break we got our safety glasses and gloves. I showed Carlos how to do his job. Then I said, "There's a lot to learn, Carlos. Do you have any questions?" Carlos said, "No. I think I understand everything, Joe. I'm ready to get to work."

Comprehension

A. Circle the letter of the correct answer(s). There may be one or two answers for each sentence.

1. Joe got Carlos a job in the _____ department.
   a. housekeeping
   b. maintenance
   c. assembly

2. At the factory, they make parts for _____ .
   a. cars
   b. planes
   c. trucks

3. Joe and Carlos wear _____ in the assembly department.
   a. gloves and safety glasses
   b. gloves and earmuffs
   c. gloves and hair nets

4. Some machines are _____ .
   a. friendly
   b. noisy
   c. nervous

5. Joe talked to Carlos about _____ .
   a. benefits
   b. safety
   c. his job

B. Number the sentences from 1 to 6 to show the correct order.

_____ Joe and Carlos took a coffee break.

_____ Joe showed Carlos the safety gear and equipment.

_____ Carlos is ready to work.

_____ Joe got Carlos a job at the factory.

_____ Joe showed Carlos how to do his job.

_____ Joe told Carlos about the safety rules.

Vocabulary

A. Complete the reading with these words or phrases.

harmful	respirator	safety rules
mask	safety gear	training

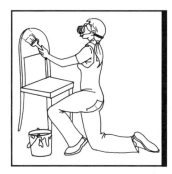

Nina is a new worker at a furniture factory. She

works in the painting and sanding department.

She is learning about her job. Nina is in

_____ . She has to learn

    1

_____ . She has to wear _____ .

    2   3

Sometimes Nina uses a sander. There is a lot of dust. She has to wear a

_____ . Sometimes Nina uses paint. Then she wears a

    4

_____ . The fumes from the paint can be _____ .

    5   6

Nina needs to remember everything. She wants to be safe at work.

B. Find and circle these words. Some words go across. Some words go down.

b	s	a	f	e	t	y	p	t
e	a	c	r	u	l	e	s	r
l	s	d	e	f	p	a	g	a
t	s	u	y	u	a	r	e	i
w	e	a	r	m	r	m	a	n
o	m	i	k	e	t	u	r	i
r	b	t	n	s	s	f	o	n
p	l	m	a	s	k	f	h	g
a	y	g	l	a	s	s	e	s

assembly   mask

belt   parts

earmuffs   rules

fumes   safety

gear   training

glasses   wear

Language Skills

Past Tense			
I	worked	we	worked
you	worked	you	worked
he she it }	worked	they	worked

A. Complete each sentence with the correct verb form.

1. (need) Carlos _____ to get a different job.

2. (help) Joe _____ Carlos get a job at his company.

3. (talk) Joe _____ to Carlos about safety rules.

4. (show) Joe _____ Carlos the safety gear.

Past Tense Questions						
Did	I	work?		Did	we	work?
Did	you	work?		Did	you	work?
Did	{ he she it	work?		Did	they	work?

B. Complete each question with the correct verb form. Then answer the questions. Use the short-answer form.

Example: Did you cook dinner last night? <u>Yes, I did.</u> *or* <u>No, I didn't.</u>

1. (work) _____ you _____ overtime yesterday? _____ .

2. (show) _____ Joe _____ Carlos the fire extinguishers? _____ .

3. (wear) _____ you _____ safety gear yesterday? _____ .

4. (get) _____ Rosa _____ a job at the factory? _____ .

🎧 Listening Practice

A. Listen to these words that end in *ed*. How many parts do you hear? Write the number.

Examples: waited <u>2</u>   talked <u>1</u>

1. lived _____
2. used _____
3. started _____
4. finished _____

5. cleaned _____
6. wanted _____
7. worked _____
8. needed _____

9. washed _____
10. loaded _____
11. punched _____
12. walked _____

B. Practice saying these words.

🎧 Reading Practice

A. Read the following poem about wearing safety gear.

How are you doing?
I'm doing just fine.
Where are you working?
On an assembly line.

What are you making?
Doors, big and small.
How is it going?
Not bad at all.

What are you wearing?
Gloves, glasses, and more.
I have to be careful
when making a door.

I wear safety gear eight hours a day.
I protect myself in every way.
I want to live, to work, to play,
to have fun in my life, and get all my pay.

B. Read the following story.

Marta works in a warehouse. There are rules for wearing safety gear. Marta works in a hard-hat area. She has to wear a hard hat. Today Marta came to work late. After she punched in, she started to work. She didn't put on her hard hat. Her co-worker Hakim saw her. He said to Marta, "Where's your hard hat?" Marta answered, "Why don't you mind your own business?"

Hakim told the boss that Marta wasn't wearing a hard hat. The boss was mad. He said to Marta, "You have to wear your safety gear all the time. You can lose your job if you don't."

Marta was mad at Hakim. She said to him, "You got me in trouble. Next time, mind your own business." Hakim said, "I just didn't want you to get hurt, Marta."

C. Discuss the following questions. Give reasons for your answers.

1. Is it important for Marta to wear her safety gear?

2. Was it OK for Hakim to tell Marta to put on her hard hat?

3. How did Marta answer Hakim? Was this a good answer? What is a better way for Marta to answer Hakim?

4. Was it OK for Hakim to talk to the boss about Marta?

🎧 More Practice: Listening

Sometimes a co-worker tells you what to do. What do you say? Listen to the dialogues. Circle the letter of the correct answer.

1. a. Thanks. I forgot.　　　　　　**b.** I don't need them.

2. a. You're not my boss. You can't tell me what to do.　　**b.** I know. I have to get a new pair.

3. a. I'll go get it.　　　　　　**b.** I'll put it on later.

4. a. Oh, thanks. I forgot it.　　　　**b.** It's OK. The boss isn't here today.

More Practice: Reading

Read the following safety rules.

SAFETY RULES

✔ Know where emergency exits are.
✔ Know where fire extinguishers are.
✔ Keep your work area neat and clean.
✔ Keep paint containers covered.
✔ Clean up all spills immediately.
✔ Store equipment safely.
✔ Bend your knees when lifting something heavy.
  Get help if you need it.
✔ Wash hands with soap and water before returning to work.
✔ Report any safety problems to your team leader or supervisor.

Discussion

1. Where are the emergency exits where you work?

2. Where are the fire extinguishers where you work?

3. Where do you store equipment and supplies at work?

4. Do you keep your work area clean?

5. What do you do if you spill something at work?

6. Do you know how to lift something heavy? Show your class.

7. What are the safety rules where you work?

8. Do all the workers follow the safety rules? Explain.

Application

1. Ask your supervisor for the safety rules where you work, or copy the rules on a piece of paper. Share them with your class.

2. Think about how to make your workplace safer. What can your employer do? What can you do? Write your suggestion.

3. Do you have a suggestion box at work? Put your suggestion on a piece of paper.

LESSON 11
Accidents Can Happen

Joe's Story

What safety problems do you see in the pictures?
Are there safety problems where you work?
Do you have accidents where you work? Explain.

🎧 **Words for Work**

accident	first-aid kit
apron	goggles
boots	protect/protective
chemical	Workers' Compensation

🎧 **More Words**

burn	procedure
careful/careless	serious
injury	spill
prevent	treat

Most of the time everyone tries to prevent accidents at work. But sometimes accidents happen. Some workers use heavy equipment and big machines. Others use dangerous chemicals. Everyone has to be careful.

We had an accident in the machine shop this morning. George was cleaning a machine. He wasn't wearing gloves. Gloves protect the hands. George spilled a chemical on his right hand. A chemical burn can be very dangerous. It needs to be washed with water immediately. At the factory there is a procedure for treating chemical burns. This morning everyone knew what to do. One person got some water. Another person got the first-aid kit. Then another worker called the supervisor. The supervisor in this department is Boris. He brought George to the emergency room. The doctor treated the burn. Then George went home. He can't work for two weeks.

Everyone feels bad about the accident. Boris was very upset because George wasn't wearing gloves. Everyone in his department has to wear gloves, boots, goggles, and an apron. They know that protective gear can prevent serious injuries. This morning George was careless.

Last week there was an accident in the assembly department. Kamel injured his eye. His goggles broke, and he didn't get new ones. Kamel got a small piece of metal in his eye. A doctor took out the piece of metal. Kamel was lucky. His eye is going to be OK. Kamel can come back to work soon. But sometimes workers get hurt and are out for a long time. They collect Workers' Compensation. It helps with medical bills and lost pay.

After an accident, everyone is careful for a while. But sometimes we are very busy. We get careless. Accidents happen. Everyone needs to be careful all the time.

Comprehension

A. Answer the following questions.

George's Accident

1. When was the accident? _____

2. Where was the accident? _____

3. Why did the accident happen? _____

_____

Kamel's Accident

1. When was the accident? _____

2. Where was the accident? _____

3. Why did the accident happen? _____

_____

B. Number the sentences from 1 to 6 to show the correct order.

_____ George went to the emergency room.

_____ George spilled a chemical on his hand.

_____ A worker got some water.

_____ The doctor treated the burn.

_____ George was cleaning a machine.

_____ A worker called the supervisor.

Vocabulary

A. Complete each sentence with one of these words.

burn	prevent	Workers' Compensation
goggles	procedure	

1. You can get a _____ from fire and from chemicals.

2. _____ prevent eye injuries.

3. You can _____ accidents by wearing safety gear.

4. There is an accident at work. Is there a _____ to follow?

5. You can get _____ when you are injured and out of work for a long time.

B. Write the correct vocabulary word or phrase on the lines. Put one letter on each line. Write the circled letters on the lines at the bottom. What word does this spell?

1. Something to protect your hands.   g __ __ __ __⊖

2. Something to protect the front of your body.   ⊖__ __ __ __

3. Something to hold emergency medical supplies.   ⊖__ __ __ __   __ __ __

      __ __ __

4. Something to protect your eyes.   __ __ __ __ __⊖ __

5. Something to protect your feet.   __ __ __⊖__

6. A hurt from an accident.   __ __ __ __ __⊖

__ __ __ __ __ __

Language Skills

Complete the reading with the past form of the following irregular verbs.

Past Tense of Irregular Verbs		
Present / Past	**Present / Past**	**Present / Past**
break / broke	go / went	put / put
do / did	is / was / were	say / said
give /gave	make / made	take / took

Pensri worked in a Thai restaurant. She

_____ a good job. One day there
    (1. do)

_____ an accident. Someone
    (2. is)

_____ a box in front of the door. Pensri
    (3. put)

didn't see it. She fell. Pensri _____ her arm. Her boss
    (4. break)

_____ her to the hospital. The doctor _____ her
    (5. take)   (6. give)

medicine for pain.

Two months later Pensri _____ back to work. Her co-workers
    (7. go)

_____ happy to see her. They _____ a big cake for
    (8. is)   (9. make)

her. They _____ , "Welcome back, Pensri. We missed you!"
    (10. say)

🎧 Oral Practice: Pronunciation

Practice the two sounds of the letter *g*. Say the following words.

gear	again	badge	danger
glasses	begin	large	emergency
gloves	earplugs	wage	manager
goggles	single	sponge	message

Do you know other words with *g*?

🎧 Reading Practice

Read the following story. Then answer the questions.

Angelo Cabral works in the welding department at Goodwin Products.

On August 16 he had an accident. At 2:30 in the afternoon Angelo was in his work area. He was pushing a heavy cart. A metal pipe fell off the cart and onto his foot. He broke his foot. Angelo reported the accident to his supervisor, Guy Le Blanc.

1. Who had an accident? _____

2. Where was the accident? _____

3. When did the accident take place? _____

Writing Practice

```
                        ACCIDENT REPORT
                        (Report of Injury)
   Please print.

   1. Employee Name _____
                          (Last)         (First)      (Middle Initial)

   2. Department _____    3. Supervisor _____

   4. Date of Accident _____    5. Time of Accident _____

   6. Location of Accident _____

   7. How Accident Happened _____

      _____

      _____

   8. Type of Injury (e.g., burn, cut, fracture) _____

      _____

   9. Name of Person to Whom Injury Was Reported _____
```

Discussion

1. Are there accidents at your workplace? Explain.
2. Do you have a first-aid kit at work? Where is it?
3. Do you have a safety procedure for accidents? What is it?
4. How do you report an accident? Do you tell someone? Do you fill out a form?

Application

1. What is in your first-aid kit at work? Make a list of everything, and bring it to class.
2. Bring an accident form to class. Fill it out. Your teacher will give you the information to use.

LESSON 12
Reporting a Problem
Joe's Story

Do you report problems at work?
How do you report a problem? Do you tell your boss? Do you
write a note? Do you fill out a form?

 Words for Work

breakdown	report
operate/operator	safety switch
OSHA	temperature
Quality Control	tools

 More Words

mistake	repair
pass/fail	responsible
pipe	toxic
plug/unplug	turn on/turn off

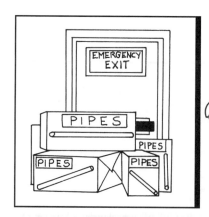

I'm a team leader. I like my job. I'm responsible for many different things. I check the equipment and machines. I look for problems. Sometimes I repair things. I carry screwdrivers, pliers, and other tools in my tool belt. But I can't fix everything. Then I have to call for help.

Sometimes there is a breakdown. This morning Pushpa, one of the machine operators, had a problem with her machine. The warning light came on. She didn't turn off the machine. She didn't tell anyone. This was a big mistake. The machine stopped. I unplugged it and called for help. It took two hours to fix her machine.

Sometimes there are safety problems. Last week there were some boxes of pipes in front of the emergency exit. At the end of the shift, the boxes were still there. Nobody reported them. This was a safety hazard. The other day I found some nails on the floor. Nobody picked up the nails or reported the problem. Someone could fall and get hurt. There are other problems, too. Sometimes there is a broken safety switch on a machine. Sometimes the temperature is too high. All these things are dangerous. There could be an accident. We also could fail a safety inspection. OSHA checks safety and health at the factory. It's important to pass these inspections.

Sometimes there are problems with supplies and materials. We have to report these problems to a supervisor. Bad materials make bad products. There is a Quality Control (QC) department. QC inspects products before they leave the factory.

At the factory we want to prevent breakdowns and accidents. We want to pass safety inspections. We want to make good products. All of us need to help. Reporting a problem is everyone's responsibility.

Comprehension

A. Circle the letter of the correct answer(s). There may be one or two answers for each sentence.

1. Joe is a team leader. He _____ .
   a. looks for problems
   b. gives out work orders
   c. checks equipment and machines

2. Joe uses _____ to do his job.
   a. spoons
   b. mops
   c. tools

3. Pushpa's machine stopped. Joe _____ .
   a. found a screwdriver
   b. unplugged the machine
   c. called for help

4. _____ is a safety hazard.
   a. A tool belt
   b. A broken safety switch
   c. A box in front of the emergency exit

5. At the factory they want to _____ .
   a. make good products
   b. make mistakes
   c. prevent accidents and breakdowns

B. Answer the following questions.

1. What was Pushpa's big mistake? _____

_____

2. Sometimes there are safety problems at Joe's factory. What are they?

_____

_____

3. It's important to report bad materials and supplies. Why? _____

_____

Vocabulary

Fill in the crossword puzzle with the correct words.

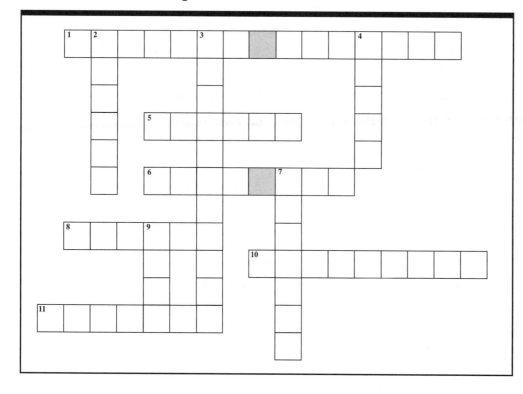

breakdown

mistake

operate

OSHA

Quality Control

repair

report

temperature

tools

turn off

unplug

Across

1. _____ checks products before they leave the factory.
5. To _____ something is to fix something.
6. To stop the oven, you _____ the oven.
8. You tell your boss about a problem. You _____ the problem.
10. A machine stops working. This is a _____ .
11. When you do something wrong you make a _____ .

Down

2. Take the plug out of the wall. _____ it.
3. The _____ of a machine should not be too high.
4. You use _____ to fix things.
7. I am a machine operator. I _____ a machine.
9. _____ inspects safety at the factory.

Language Skills

Complete the reading with the past form of the following irregular verbs.

Past Tense of Irregular Verbs		
Present / Past	**Present / Past**	**Present / Past**
bring/brought	have/had	see/saw
find/found	leave/left	shut/shut
get/got	lose/lost	tell/told

My name is Stella Lobo. I'm a floor supervisor at the Fairlane Nursing Home. I work the second shift. Last night I

_____ a lot of problems. First
(1. have)

I _____ three people smoking in the building. Then I
(2. see)

_____ the keys to the storage room. I couldn't get
(3. lose)

the supplies. After that one of the workers _____ the
(4. bring)

wrong meals to the patients.

I had to fix all the problems. I _____ the workers
(5. tell)

to stop smoking. I _____ keys to the storage room. I
(6. find)

_____ the meals.
(7. get)

By 6:00 I had a headache. I _____ the floor and
(8. leave)

went to the kitchen. I _____ the door and
(9. shut)

_____ a cup of coffee. It was good to take a
(10. get)

break. After that I was ready for more problems.

🎧 Oral Practice: Dialogue

**Practice reporting a problem. Use your supervisor's name
for the first blank below. Use your name for the second blank.
Practice with a partner. Then write your own dialogues.**

EMPLOYEE: ___(your supervisor's name)___, this is ___(your name)___ . There's smoke in
the storage room.

SUPERVISOR: Call 911. I'll be right there.

EMPLOYEE: ___(your supervisor's name)___, this is ___(your name)___ . We have a
problem. The new material didn't come in. We can't finish the job.

SUPERVISOR: OK. I'll be right there.

EMPLOYEE: _____

_____ .

SUPERVISOR: _____ .

🎧 Listening Practice

Listen to the problems. Circle the letter of the best answer.

1. a. Nothing.   **b.** Tell her supervisor.   **c.** Call 911.

2. a. Call the fire   **b.** Tell his friend.   **c.** Go back to work.
department.

3. a. Use any material.   **b.** Find her supervisor   **c.** Ask her friend.
and ask.

4. a. Nothing.   **b.** Clean it up.   **c.** Call housekeeping.

5. a. Tell his boss.   **b.** Tell his co-worker.   **c.** Start working.

98 Lesson 12

🎧 Reading Practice

Read the following story. Then answer the questions.

Edna and Flor are friends. They work together cleaning houses. Last week Edna was cleaning a bathroom. She mixed ammonia and bleach together. The fumes were toxic. They made her sick.

Edna had trouble breathing. Flor was scared. What could she do? She called 911. Her English wasn't very good. Flor was very nervous, but she did it! She talked to the dispatcher and gave him the necessary information.

The ambulance came immediately and took Edna to County Hospital. Edna was very lucky because Flor was able to call for help. Flor saved her friend's life!

1. Who are Edna and Flor? _____

2. What happened to Edna? _____

3. When did it happen? _____

4. How did Flor save Edna's life? _____

Application

1. There are many kinds of emergencies. Make a list with your class.

2. Practice reporting an emergency. Complete the form and read it to the class. Speak clearly so everyone can understand you.

My name is _____ .

I live at _____ .

I need help. (Explain the emergency.) _____

_____

UNIT 4
Ramón's Story

The U.S. Workplace

LESSON 13
Laid Off

Ramón's Story

How did you find your job?
Did you look on a bulletin board?

 Words for Work

apply/application	laid off/layoff	temporary	bulletin board
available	permanent	Unemployment Office	depressed
help wanted ads	reference	wage	slow down
job opening	salary	work experience	worried

 More Words

My name is Ramón Rivera. I am Joe Garcia's brother-in-law. My wife, Ana, and Joe's wife, Maria, are sisters. Ana and I came to the U.S. about three years ago. I got a job at a building supply company. It was a good job. I made good money.

About three months ago work slowed down. People at the company started talking about a layoff. Everyone was nervous.

Then in April I was laid off. I was out of work for almost three months. I had a hard time finding a job. I didn't know what to do. I talked to Joe. I talked to my friends and neighbors. I went to the stores in my neighborhood. I also went to the Unemployment Office. I looked at the bulletin boards. I looked at the help wanted ads in the newspaper, too. I looked for job openings. I tried to find permanent or temporary work. I filled out a lot of applications. I couldn't find a job.

The layoff was hard for me. We had a lot of bills to pay. Ana had to work overtime to make more money. Her regular salary wasn't enough. I was home all day, and I didn't have anything to do. I worried all the time about getting another job. I was depressed. It was difficult for everyone in the family.

One day I saw a help wanted sign in a store window. I went inside the store to apply for the job. First I filled out an application. I wrote down information about my education and work experience. I gave the names of two references. Then I talked to the manager, Ms. Lee. She asked me some questions. She asked about my last job. I told her about the layoff. Next Ms. Lee took me around the store. She told me about the job. Then she said, "This is the only job available now. The wage is $10 an hour plus overtime. Do you want the job?" I said, "Yes, I do! When can I start?" Ms. Lee said, "I'll call you in a few days. First I have to check your references."

Now I have to wait for Ms. Lee to call. I hope I don't have to wait too long. I really need this job.

Comprehension

A. Circle the letter of the correct answer(s). There may be one or two answers for each sentence.

1. There was a layoff at the company because _____ .
   a. work slowed down
   b. work was good
   c. the assembly department closed

2. When he was out of work, Ramón _____ .
   a. went to school
   b. looked for a new job
   c. was depressed

3. The layoff was _____ .
   a. difficult for everyone in the family
   b. good for Ana
   c. easy

4. Ramón wrote about his _____ on the job application.
   a. work experience
   b. family
   c. education

5. Ms. Lee asked Ramón _____ .
   a. about his friends and neighbors
   b. about his last job
   c. about unemployment

B. Ramón tried to find a new job. What did he do? Complete the sentences.

1. He talked to _____.

2. He went to the _____.

3. He looked at the _____.

4. He filled out _____.

Vocabulary

A. Complete each sentence with one of these words or phrases.

application	temporary	wages
job opening	Unemployment Office	work experience

1. The restaurant needs a worker. There is a _____ at the restaurant.

2. You fill out an _____ for a job.

3. A job for a short time is a _____ job.

4. All your jobs make up your _____ .

5. The money you earn is your salary or your_____ .

6. You can go to the _____ when you don't have a job.

B. Find and circle these words. Some words go across. Some words go down.

w	a	v	a	i	l	a	b	l	e	a
e	p	e	r	m	a	n	e	n	t	c
h	p	o	s	r	t	l	x	p	e	r
n	l	a	y	o	f	f	p	i	m	f
r	i	w	o	r	r	i	e	d	p	a
d	c	n	w	g	l	u	r	h	o	p
s	a	l	a	r	y	p	i	g	r	e
u	t	a	g	o	m	g	e	s	a	n
f	i	k	e	t	c	o	n	l	r	b
j	o	m	s	a	f	s	c	t	y	s
a	n	r	e	f	e	r	e	n	c	e

application

available

experience

layoff

permanent

reference

salary

temporary

wages

worried

Language Skills

The prepositions *at*, *on*, and *in* are used with places.

at	number and street	*Example:* Sonia lives **at** 65 Broad Street
on	street, avenue, road, etc.	*Example:* Sonia lives **on** Broad Street
in	city, state, country	*Example:* Sonia lives **in** Austin, Texas, **in** the U.S.

Complete the sentences with *at*, *on*, or *in*.

1. Dung lives _____ 78 Western Avenue.

2. The hospital is _____ First Street.

3. Galina lived _____ Japan for two years.

4. The new supermarket is _____ Route 34.

5. My mother and father live _____ a very busy street.

6. I work _____ 65 York Avenue _____ Miami.

7. Is your sister _____ New Mexico now?

8. The nursing home is _____ Clairmont Street _____ Long Beach, California.

🎧 Oral Practice: Pronunciation

Practice the sounds of the letters *l* and *r* in the following words.

label	rag	lamp/ramp
late	recipe	lap/wrap
layoff	repair	late/rate
leak	report	lead/read
left	required	light/right
like	ride	list/wrist
lobby	room	load/road
lunch	rules	long/wrong

Do you know other words with the letters *l* and *r*?

Reading Practice

Read the following help wanted ads. Then answer the questions.

ASST. COOK
PT, THU F SAT 4-8
Will train. Latin Village
Call Lisa 775-2134

LAUNDRY WORKER
Hudson Nursing Home
FT, M-F 9-5
For more info. call Laura,
HR Dept. 354-7893

MACHINE OPERATOR
Exp. req. FT, 2nd Shift M-F
Baker Manuf. Co. $10/hr, OT possible,
Call for appt. 595-6597   Ext. 624

STORE CLERK
Women's Clothing Dept.
40 hrs/wk 2-10 pm. Good Benefits.
16 North Ave. 432-6660

DELIVERY PERSON
Immed. need PT
Mario's Pizza
Call 864-3892

1. Which jobs are part-time?

2. Which jobs are full-time?

3. Which job requires experience?

4. Lena is looking for a full-time job with good benefits. What number should she call?

5. Julia wants the job as a laundry worker. Who should she call?

6. Roberto likes to cook. Where should he apply for a job?

7. Louis wants to work full-time Monday to Friday. Which jobs may be good for him?

Writing Practice

Fill out the form below with your personal information.

APPLICATION FOR EMPLOYMENT

PERSONAL INFORMATION

Name _____
        First   Last   Middle Initial

Address _____
         Street   Apt. No.   City   State   Zip Code

Telephone _____ Social Security No. _____

Job Applied for _____ When can you start? _____

Days and Hours Available _____

WORK RECORD

Job _____   Job _____

Company _____   Company _____

Address _____   Address _____

Telephone _____   Telephone _____

Years _____   Years _____

REFERENCES

Name _____   Name _____

Address _____   Address _____

Telephone _____   Telephone _____

Relationship _____   Relationship _____

Signature _____ Date _____

More Practice: Vocabulary

Many abbreviations are used in help wanted ads. Match the abbreviations with the correct word.

1. _____ asst.   **a.** temporary
2. _____ PT   **b.** paid
3. _____ dept.   **c.** overtime
4. _____ A.M.   **d.** appointment
5. _____ info.   **e.** hour
6. _____ M-F   **f.** afternoon or evening
7. _____ wk.   **g.** morning
8. _____ appt.   **h.** required
9. _____ FT   **i.** part-time
10. _____ co.   **j.** information
11. _____ P.M.   **k.** assistant
12. _____ hr.   **l.** Monday through Friday
13. _____ pd.   **m.** full-time
14. _____ temp   **n.** week
15. _____ req'd.   **o.** company
16. _____ OT   **p.** department

More Practice: Reading

Read the following newspaper article and answer the questions.

LAYOFF AT ROME TEXTILES

ROME — Next month Rome Textiles will lay off 1,500 workers. At a meeting yesterday, Robert Lowell, president of the company, told employees about the layoff. "Work at our company has slowed down," said Mr. Lowell. "Last year we lost over $3 million. We have to close some of our departments. This is sad for all of us."

The layoff is bad news for many people. Almost 60 percent of residents in this area work at Rome Textiles. Everyone is worried about the future. "I don't know what I'm going to do," said Lenny Ripka, an employee at the factory. "I have four kids and I need a job. There's no other place to work in the area. Where can I go?"

The layoff is also bad news for many stores and businesses. Luca Rossi, owner of a retail store in Rome, said, "A layoff hurts all of us. When people are out of work, they don't spend much money. This is bad for business."

Yesterday Mr. Lowell said, "We hope this is going to be a temporary layoff. We want to get everyone back to work soon."

1. Rome Textiles is going to lay off 1,500 workers. Why?

2. Lenny Ripka is an employee of Rome Textiles. The layoff is bad for him. Why?

3. Luca Rossi is a business owner. The layoff is bad for him. Why?

Discussion

1. Were you ever laid off? How did you feel? What did you do?

2. Do people at work talk about a layoff?

Application

1. Do you have a bulletin board at work? Where is it?

2. What is on your bulletin board? Tell your class.

LESSON 14
At the Store

Ramón's Story

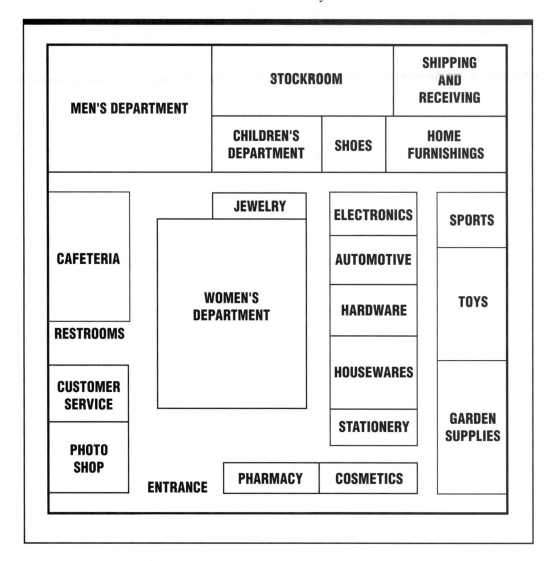

Do you know all of these departments in a store?
Do you know the departments where you work?

🎧 Words for Work

damaged	item	Shipping and Receiving
deliveries	load/unload	stock/restock/stockroom
dolly	pack/unpack	union
dues	price	

🎧 More Words

container
heavy
join
meeting

I got the job at the store. I started working three weeks ago. I work in the stockroom. I also work on the floor. There's a lot to do. I only sit down at break and at lunch. Some days I'm very tired, but I like to be busy. It's good to be working again.

The store sells clothes, tools, furniture, and other things. There are many departments. It's a big store. Deliveries come in every day. The deliveries go to Shipping and Receiving. Workers in Shipping and Receiving unload the trucks and bring the boxes to the stockroom. I unpack the boxes and check everything. I put damaged items in a big container. I use a dolly or cart to move heavy things. I don't want to hurt my back. Some days I restock the shelves. I also put prices on all the items. The store has a sale every week. The sale prices have to be correct.

There are a lot of new things to get used to at the store. There's even a union here. Last night I went to a meeting for new workers. One of the union members talked to us. His name is Larry. Larry talked about the union. He told us about the benefits and the dues. He said, "The union helps workers get better pay. Sometimes it can also help employees with problems." Larry gave us some information to read at home. I don't understand everything. Maybe my brother-in-law can help me. I need to think about joining the union.

Sometimes I miss my old job. I knew a lot of people, and I was comfortable there. But I like this job. There are a lot of good things about working here. The store is near my apartment. I can walk to work. The benefits are good. I work overtime, too. Last week I worked five hours overtime. It was good to have the extra money. We have a lot of bills to pay. I was out of work for a long time. I hope I keep this job for a while. I never want to be laid off again.

Comprehension

A. Circle the letter of the correct answer(s). There may be one or two answers for each sentence.

1. Ramón sits down _____ .
   a. all day
   b. at lunch
   c. at break

2. The store sells _____ .
   a. clothes
   b. tools
   c. carts

3. Workers in Shipping and Receiving _____ .
   a. unload the trucks
   b. put prices on the items
   c. bring the items to the floor

4. Every week there is _____ at the store.
   a. a party
   b. a sale
   c. a layoff

5. It is good for Ramón to be working again because _____ .
   a. he has to lift heavy things
   b. he has to pay his bills
   c. he likes to be busy

B. Ramón likes working at the store. Why? Check the reasons.

1. _____ He can walk to work.

2. _____ He doesn't have to do a lot.

3. _____ He has good benefits.

4. _____ He works overtime.

5. _____ He has a nice boss.

6. _____ He likes to be busy.

7. _____ He works with his friends.

Vocabulary

Complete the reading with these words.

container	dolly	meeting	stockroom
damaged	dues	prices	unload
deliveries	join	stock	

Rollins Department Store is a big place.

New _____ come in every

1

day. The trucks bring the items to Shipping

and Receiving. The workers in Shipping and

Receiving _____ the trucks.

2

The workers in the _____ unpack the boxes.

3

Sometimes they have to use a _____ to move heavy

4

items. Some items are no good. These things are

_____ . The workers put these items in a big

5

_____ . Other workers _____ the

6   7

shelves and put _____ on the items.

8

There is a union at the store. Any worker can

_____ the union, but it costs money. Union members

9

pay _____ every week. Tonight there is a big

10

_____ for all new union members. They are going

11

to talk about wages. It is important for everyone to go.

Language Skills

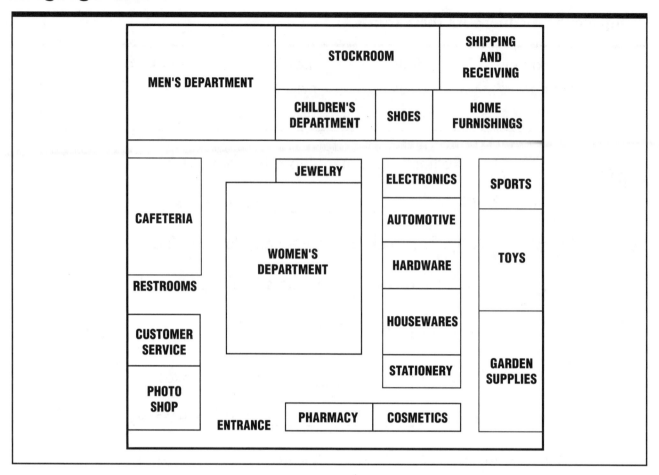

Pretend you are at the store entrance. Complete each sentence.

across from	in the back/front of	next to	on the left/right

Example: Shipping and Receiving is <u>next to</u> the stockroom.

1. The Shoe Department is _____ Home Furnishings.

2. Jewelry is _____ the Children's Department.

3. The Men's Department is _____ the store.

4. Electronics is _____ Shoes.

5. The restrooms are _____ side of the store. They are _____ Customer Service.

6. Hardware is _____ side of the store, _____ Toys.

🎧 Listening Practice

Look at the map on page 114. Listen carefully. Where are you?
Circle the letter of the correct answer.

1. **a.** Pharmacy   **b.** Garden Supplies   **c.** Photo Shop

2. **a.** Restrooms   **b.** Customer Service   **c.** Cafeteria

3. **a.** Women's Department   **b.** Shoes   **c.** Children's Department

4. **a.** Hardware   **b.** Electronics   **c.** Sports

5. **a.** Housewares   **b.** Pharmacy   **c.** Stationery

Reading Practice

Read the following story. Then answer the questions.

My name is Luz. I am 48 years

old. I came to the U.S. 15 years ago. For many years I stayed home with my two children. I was on welfare. I went to ESL class.

Then the law changed. I had to get a job. I was nervous. I was afraid my English wasn't good enough. My daughter helped me get a job in a store.

We both work there.

I like my job. I stock the shelves and keep things in order. Sometimes people ask me questions. I try to help them. I like to help people. I also like to get my paycheck.

This job is important to me. It makes me feel good. This job is also important for my children. They see me work hard, and so they work hard, too.

1. Why did Luz have to get a job? _____

2. Why does Luz like her job? _____

3. Why is Luz's job important to her? _____

4. Why is Luz's job important for her children? _____

More Practice: Language

Look at the store map on page 114. Where are other departments in the store? Practice questions and answers with a partner.

Example: <u>Where is Housewares?</u>   <u>Housewares is next to Stationery.</u>

Cultural Exchange

1. Do you have unions in your native country?
2. Do you have a union where you work in the U.S.? Do you belong? Why or why not?

Application

1. There are many departments in a store. Are there departments where you work? What are they?
2. Make a map of your department or workplace.
3. What things are good about your job? Make a list.

LESSON 15
Getting Along with Sam
Ramón's Story

Do you talk to everyone at work? Why or why not?
Do you get along with everyone at work? Why or why not?

 Words for Work

amount	Human Resources (HR)	quantity
assistant	instructions	raise
Customer Service	inventory	review
get along with	promotion	

 More Words

figure it out
list
repeat
yell

When I started my job at the store, I didn't know any of the other workers. No one spoke my language. But most of the people were nice. They helped me find things. We had coffee break and lunch together. They made me feel comfortable.

One guy was hard to get along with. His name is Sam. Sam wasn't friendly. Most of the time he didn't even look at me. One day Sam and I had to work together. Sam didn't talk to me. When I asked him a question, he said, "Go figure it out yourself! I have my own work to do." Last month the manager told Sam to show me how to take inventory. Sam told me to count all the items and put the total amount on the inventory list under *quantity*. Sam spoke very fast. I had to ask him to repeat the instructions. He yelled, "What's wrong with you? Where do you come from? Can't you understand English?"

Sam makes me mad. He makes me feel stupid. I know my English isn't great, but I'm not stupid! I need to understand. I want to do a good job. I don't know what to say to Sam, so I stay away from him.

Today Sam got a promotion. He is the new assistant manager. Now Sam and I are going to work together every day. He is going to do the work schedules. He is going to give me instructions every morning. He is going to report any problems to the manager, Ms. Lee. Next month I'm going to have my review. I'm worried about it. I want a good review so I can get a raise. I have to get along with Sam.

Maybe I should talk to Sam. Maybe I should talk to the manager. I don't know what to do. I can't go to Human Resources. We don't have a department like that at the store. I want to do the right thing. Tonight I'm going to talk to my brother-in-law, Joe. I hope he can tell me what to do. Maybe he can help me figure out how to get along with Sam.

Comprehension

A. Circle the letter of the correct answer(s). There may be one or two answers for each sentence.

1. When Ramón came to the store, most of the workers _____ .
   a. were nice
   b. yelled at him
   c. made him feel comfortable

2. Sam wasn't _____ .
   a. fast
   b. mad
   c. friendly

3. Sam was promoted to _____ .
   a. manager
   b. assistant manager
   c. supervisor

4. Ramón has to get along with Sam because _____ .
   a. he is going to work with him every day
   b. he wants a good review
   c. he wants a new friend

5. Ramón doesn't know what to do about Sam. Maybe he should _____ .
   a. get a new job
   b. talk to the manager
   c. talk to Sam

B. Finish the story.

Ramón talks to his brother-in-law, Joe, about his problem with Sam. What do you think Joe says? Work with a partner and finish the story. Then share your story with the class.

Vocabulary

A. Complete each sentence with one of these words or phrases.

| Customer Service | get along with | raise |
| figure it out | Human Resources | review |

1. You buy something at a store. There is a problem. You go to
_____ for help.

2. I don't always understand what people say, but I try to
_____ .

3. My boss told me that I was doing a good job. I had a good
_____ .

4. I don't want to fight with my co-workers. I want to _____
them.

5. You work hard. You get more money. You get a _____ .

6. Employees can go to the _____ Department for help.

B. Match each word with the correct meaning.

____ 1. assistant   **a.** say or do again

____ 2. yell   **b.** a better job; higher position at work

____ 3. inventory   **c.** more money; an increase in pay

____ 4. repeat   **d.** a helper

____ 5. instructions   **e.** amount

____ 6. promotion   **f.** shout; talk loudly

____ 7. raise   **g.** directions

____ 8. quantity   **h.** a list of items in a store; stock

Language Skills

Future Tense						
Full Form	**Contraction**			**Full Form**	**Contraction**	
I am	(I'm)	going to work		we are	(we're)	going to work
you are	(you're)	going to work		you are	(you're)	going to work
he is	(he's)	going to work				
she is	(she's)	going to work		they are	(they're)	going to work
it is	(it's)	going to work				

A. Complete each sentence with the correct verb form.

Example: (work) Selma <u>is going to work</u> overtime on Saturday.

1. (take) I _____ a day off tomorrow.

2. (apply) Raj _____ for a new job next week.

3. (cut) They _____ the carpet after lunch.

4. (set up) We _____ the conference room this afternoon.

Future Tense Negative						
I'm	not	going to	work	we	aren't	going to work
you	aren't	going to	work	you	aren't	going to work
he she it }	isn't	going to	work	they	aren't	going to work

B. Complete each sentence with the negative form of the verb.

Example: (take) <u>I'm not going to take</u> a break this afternoon.

1. (get) Sam _____ a promotion this year.

2. (finish) We _____ the job today.

3. (take) I _____ my vacation in July next year.

Unit 4 Ramón's Story 121

🎧 Reading Practice

A. Read the following poem about Ramón and Sam.

I work with many people
each and every day.
Most say, "Hi, how are you?"
But Sam looks away.

Sam doesn't talk to me.
I really don't know why.
I'm a pretty nice person.
I'm just a regular guy.

I know my face is different
and I have a different name.
But I want to say to Sam
we are very much the same.

**B. Now read about another problem with co-workers. This is Mon's story.
Read her story. Then answer the questions.**

My name is Mon. I work on a team
with two other people. These two people
come from the same country, and they
speak the same language. They don't talk
to me very much, but they talk to each
other all day. I do most of the work. This
makes me mad. The boss doesn't know.
I don't know what to do.

1. What is Mon's problem? _____

2. What should she do? _____

3. Do you have any problems with your co-workers? _____

4. What should you do? _____

More Practice: Reading

Stockroom Inventory			
Qty	Item Description	Stock No.	Unit Price
28	trash can-plastic 9 gal. w/cover	IL123	$12.75
33	trash can-plastic 9 gal. w/o cover	IL124	$10.75
18	trash can-plastic 12 gal. w/cover	IL125	$15.25
11	trash can-plastic 12 gal. w/o cover	IL126	$13.25
38	sheet-single-white-fitted	S40S	$9.75
42	sheet-single-white-flat	S41S	$10.50
44	sheet-double-white-fitted	S42D	$11.25
26	sheet-double-white-flat	S43D	$12.00
33	sheet-queen-white-fitted	S44Q	$13.25
29	sheet-queen-white-flat	S45Q	$13.50
18	sheet-king-white-fitted	S46K	$15.35
16	sheet-king-white-flat	S47K	$15.00

Look at the Stockroom Inventory above. Then answer the following questions.

1. The Sunshine Motel needs 30 of item # S44Q and 30 of item # S45Q. What items do they need to buy? _____ What is the total amount of the sale? _____

2. Hope Manufacturing Company wants to order ten 12-gallon trash cans with covers and eight 9-gallon trash cans without covers. How much will they pay for the trash cans? _____

3. County Hospital needs 60 single white fitted sheets and 60 single white flat sheets. There aren't enough sheets in the stockroom. How many fitted sheets does the store have to order? _____ How many flat sheets? _____ What is the total cost of the sheets the store needs to order? _____

More Practice: Language Skills

Ask a partner the following questions. Tell the class your partner's answers.

Example: What are you going to do tomorrow?   <u>I'm going to ask for a raise.</u>

1. What are you going to do tomorrow?   _____

2. What are you going to do next week?   _____

3. What are you going to do next weekend?   _____

4. What are you going to do next summer?   _____

5. What are you going to do in a few years?   _____

Application

Take an inventory of things in a room at the place where you work (storage room, work area, cafeteria, etc.) or in your classroom. Use or copy the form below for your inventory.

INVENTORY OF	
Qty.	Item
_____	_____
_____	_____
_____	_____
_____	_____
_____	_____
_____	_____

LESSON 16
Understanding the U.S.

Ramón's Story

Are you a good worker? Do you need new job skills?
Is it hard to work in the U.S.? Is it hard to understand
everything about the U.S.?

 Words for Work

attendance	excellent	Performance Evaluation
computer	hardworking	punctual
cooperative	improve	skills
dependable	neat	

 More Words

citizen

copy

dictionary

It takes a long time to feel comfortable in a new country. It takes a long time to feel comfortable at work. Every place is different. There is so much to learn.

Last week I had my review at work. This was my first review in the U.S. My manager called me into her office. She said, "Ramón, I'm very happy with your work. Your attendance is excellent. You're punctual. You're hardworking. You're a very dependable worker. I'm going to give you a raise." This was good news! Then Ms. Lee gave me the review to read. It was hard to understand. There were a lot of words I didn't know. I didn't know the words *Performance Evaluation*, *cooperative*, and *neat*. I took a copy of the review home. Everyone in my family tried to help me. We looked up some words in the dictionary. This was good for all of us. We need to learn new words.

We need to learn many other things about work. We don't always know what to say or do. For example, is it OK to correct the boss when he makes a mistake? What do we do when we make a mistake? My wife, Ana, wants to ask for a raise. What does she say to her boss?

We also need to learn other things about this country. We want to know the right thing to do. For example, what do we bring to a birthday party? What do we wear to a wedding? What do we say when someone dies?

Maria, Joe, Ana, and I talk about many things. We try to figure out what to say and do. We want to understand everything about the U.S. We have a good life here, but we still have a lot to learn. Next month Joe and I are going to take a computer class. Computer skills are important in this country. Ana is going to start an ESL class in a few weeks. She wants to improve her English. We want to become U.S. citizens. We want to be a part of this country. The U.S. is our home now.

Comprehension

A. Circle the letter of the correct answer(s). There may be one or two answers for each sentence.

1. Ramón is a good worker because _____ .
   a. he comes to work on time
   b. he is cooperative
   c. he takes a lot of vacations

2. Ms. Lee gave Ramón _____ .
   a. a promotion
   b. a raise
   c. a review

3. Ramón still has a lot to learn. Next month he and Joe are going to _____ .
   a. take an ESL class
   b. take a citizenship class
   c. take a computer class

4. Maria, Joe, Ana, and Ramón want to become U.S. citizens because _____ .
   a. the U.S. is their home now
   b. they want to be a part of this country
   c. they like their jobs

B. Answer the following questions.

1. Did Ramón have a good review? Explain. _____

_____

2. Ramón needs to learn many things about work. He also needs to learn

many things about the U.S. Why is this important to Ramón? _____

_____

Vocabulary

**Write the correct vocabulary word on the lines. Put one letter on
each line. Write the circled letters on the lines at the bottom.
What word does this spell?**

1. Lola works well with other
   people. She is _____ .

   C __ __ __ __ Ⓞ __ __ __ __ __

2. Monique did a great job today.
   Her work was _____ .

   Ⓞ __ __ __ __ __ __ __ __ __

3. Ali needs to do a better job.
   His work needs to _____ .

   __ __ __ __ __ Ⓞ __

4. Edvar's boss told him he was
   doing a good job. He gave
   Edvar a good Performance

   _____ .

   __ __ __ __ __ __ Ⓞ __ __

5. Pravit's work station is never
   messy. It is always _____ .

   __ Ⓞ __ __

6. Yoshi works hard all day. She
   is _____ .

   __ __ __ __ Ⓞ __ __ __ __ __

   __ __ __ __ __ __

Language Skills

Future Tense Questions							
Am	I	going to	work?	Are	we	going to	work?
Are	you	going to	work?	Are	you	going to	work?
Is	he / she / it	going to	work?	Are	they	going to	work?

Complete each question with the correct verb form.

Example: Is your brother <u>going to apply</u> for a new job?

1. (talk) _____ you _____ to your boss about the problem?

2. (take) _____ Clara _____ the day off tomorrow?

3. (deliver) _____ they _____ the shipment this afternoon?

4. (get) _____ I _____ a raise soon?

5. (study) _____ you _____ English next year?

6. (fix) _____ we _____ the machine later?

7. (wash) _____ she _____ the floors tonight?

8. (clean up) _____ you _____ your work area?

Oral Practice: Pronunciation

Say these words. How many parts does each word have?
Write the number.

1. raise _____
2. hardworking _____
3. inventory _____
4. excellent _____

5. improve _____
6. evaluation _____
7. attendance _____
8. quantity _____

9. computer _____
10. application _____
11. skills _____
12. dependable _____

Reading Practice

A. Look at the review below. Then answer the questions.

Performance Evaluation		Excellent	Satisfactory	Needs Improvement
Name: Ping Ho	**Work**			
	Job skills		X	
	Keeps area clean and neat	X		
Job: Meat Packer	Follows instructions		X	
	Follows safety rules		X	
	Completes work on time	X		
	Asks questions when necessary			X
Supervisor Signature	Reports problems			X
Janek Huminski	**Personal Qualities**			
	Attendance	X		
Employee Signature	Punctual	X		
Ping Ho	Helpful and cooperative	X		
	Dependable	X		
Date *12/10/03*	Accepts correction			X

1. What is Ping Ho's job? _____

2. Does Ping come to work on time? _____

3. Do you think Ping *always* follows safety rules? Explain. _____

4. Does Ping speak up at work? How do you know? _____

5. Does she get along with her co-workers? _____

6. What personal quality needs improvement? _____

7. Is this a good review? What do you think? _____

B. Discuss the following questions with your classmates.

1. Ping does not accept correction well. What can she do to improve?

2. Do you accept correction well?

Writing Practice

What kind of worker are you? Use as many of the following words as you can to write about yourself.

(a)		(b)
neat	careful	ask questions
hardworking	fast	follow directions
helpful	punctual	report problems
responsible	dependable	follow safety rules
cooperative		come to work on time
		get along with my co-workers
		complete work on time
		speak English most of the time

I work at _____ . I'm a _____ . I'm a good
           (place)   (job)

worker. I'm _____ , _____ , and
           (a)   (a)

_____ . Also, I _____ , and I _____ .
   (a)   (b)   (b)

There are some things I need to improve. I need to be _____ . I
                                             (a)

also need to _____ .
          (b)

Let's Think about It

Ramón doesn't always know what to say and do at work. Read the sentences. Then answer the questions with your class.

1. You don't understand your boss. What do you say?
   a. Nothing. You just smile.
   b. "I don't understand. Please repeat that."

2. Your co-worker's father died. What do you say?
   a. Nothing.
   b. "I was sorry to hear about your father."

3. A co-worker says to you, "I like your shirt." What do you say?
   a. "Thank you."
   b. Nothing.

4. You want to work overtime. What do you do?
   a. Talk to your boss.
   b. Work overtime without talking to your boss.

5. Your partner is slow. You do most of the work. What do you do?
   a. Talk to your partner about it.
   b. Tell your boss.

6. Your boss wants to promote you. You are nervous about the work. What do you do?
   a. Talk to your boss.   **c.** Turn down the job.
   b. Take the job.

7. Your co-workers get a raise. You don't. You are upset. What do you do?
   a. Get mad at your co-workers.   **c.** Talk to your boss.
   b. Quit your job.

8. You need to ask your boss a question. He is talking to someone. What do you do?
   a. Go back to work.   **c.** Say, "Excuse me," and wait to
   b. Start talking.   speak.

9. Your co-worker gives you some food. You don't want it. What do you say?
   a. "No, thank you."   **c.** "What is this?"
   b. Nothing.

🎧 More Practice: Reading

Read about Ramón and his family. Then answer the questions.

Ana and I like it here in the U.S. We have a nice apartment. We have good jobs. We can pay our bills. Our kids are happy, too. They like school and have lots of friends.

Every Sunday we get together with Maria and Joe. We eat Mexican food. We play games. We listen to Spanish music. We watch soccer on TV. Sometimes we call our family in Mexico.

Our kids used to like Sundays. Now they don't want to stay home with the family. They want to go out with their friends. They want to eat U.S. food and listen to U.S. music. They like to go to movies and football games. They speak English most of the time. They don't want to speak Spanish. We don't want our kids to forget Spanish. We want them to be able to talk to their grandparents and other people in the family.

Our kids want to be like kids in the U.S. Ana and I want our kids to be happy, but sometimes we feel sad. We don't want them to lose our language and our culture.

1. What do Ramón and Ana do on Sunday?

2. What do their kids want to do?

3. Why do Ramón and Ana sometimes feel sad?

4. Is it important to keep your native culture?

5. Do you speak your native language at home?

6. Do you speak your native language at work?

Application

Write your story. Use Ramón's story as a model. Share your story with the class.

LISTENING EXERCISE PROMPTS

UNIT 1 LESSON 2

Application: Listening Practice (page 21)

Listen to the questions. Write your answers to the questions.

1. What country are you from?
2. What was your job in your native country?
3. When did you come to the U.S.?
4. What was your first job in the U.S.?
5. What is your telephone number?
6. What is your zip code?
7. What is your date of birth?
8. When is your ESL class?

LESSON 4

Listening Practice (page 35)

Listen to the measurements. Write what you hear. Use numerals and abbreviations.

1. two and one-half quarts
2. one hundred and eighty pounds
3. two-thirds cup
4. five thousand, one hundred forty pounds
5. three and three-fourths teaspoons
6. fifteen gallons
7. six and seven-tenths inches
8. thirteen thousand, two hundred forty feet

UNIT 2 LESSON 5

Listening Practice (page 42)

Listen to the times, days, and dates. Write what you hear.

1. Monday
2. 6:30
3. March 30th
4. 7:45 A.M.
5. July 13, 2002
6. Wednesday
7. September 21st
8. Thursday, January 11th
9. 5:15 P.M.
10. Tuesday, August 3rd
11. 10 past 4
12. April 19, 1996

LESSON 6

Listening Practice (page 51)

Following Directions

Part 1. Listen to the dialogues. Say the answers to the questions you hear.

Example:

A. Please get the bleach. It's on the bottom shelf.
B. I don't understand. Where's the bleach?
A. It's on the bottom shelf.

Now listen to the following dialogues and answer each question.

1. A. Please get the sponges. They're on the third shelf.
   B. I don't understand. Where are the sponges?
2. A. Please get the vacuum. It's in the storage room.
   B. I don't understand. Where's the vacuum?
3. A. Please get the glasses. They're on the top shelf.
   B. I don't understand. Where are the glasses?
4. A. Please get the mop. It's in the supply closet.
   B. I don't understand. Where's the mop?

Part 2. Listen to the directions. Then see if you can repeat them in the same order.

1. First, dust the bedroom.
   Next, make the bed.
   Then, vacuum the bedroom.
2. First, cut up the carrots.
   Next, cut up the potatoes.
   Then, cut up the onions.
3. First, punch in.
   Next, get a uniform.
   Then, go to the department.
   Last, get a work order.

LESSON 7

Listening Practice (page 59)

Listen to the message. Write what you hear.

Date: April 17th, two thousand three
Time: 6:00 A.M.
To: Ray Jones [r-a-y j-o-n-e-s]
From: Ana Rivera [a-n-a r-i-v-e-r-a]
Message: Lin Wu [l-i-n w-u] cannot come to work today. She is sick.

UNIT 3 LESSON 10

More Practice: Listening (page 84)

Listen to each dialogue. Circle the letter of the correct answer.

1. **A.** You should wear your safety glasses. You can get something in your eye.
   B. a. Thanks. I forgot.
      b. I don't need them.
2. **A.** You'd better get your gloves. The machine is hot.
   B. a. You're not my boss. You can't tell me what to do.
      b. I know. I have to get a new pair.
3. **A.** We're using the sander today. Where is your mask?
   B. a. I'll go get it.
      b. I'll put it on later.
4. **A.** You're supposed to wear a hair net, you know.
   B. a. Oh, thanks. I forgot it.
      b. It's OK. The boss isn't here today.

LESSON 12

Listening Practice (page 98)

Listen to the problems. Circle the letter of the best answer.

1. Magda works in a laundry. The washing machine is making a loud noise. What should Magda do?
2. Ahmad works in a restaurant. He sees smoke in the supply room. What should Ahmad do?
3. Mei Ling works in a garment factory. She doesn't know what material to use. What should Mei Ling do?
4. Judith works in a hospital. She brings meals to the patients. She sees a spill on the floor in Room 35 that could be hazardous. What should Judith do?
5. Luis works at a construction company. He found a mistake in the work order. What should he do?

UNIT 4 LESSON 14

Listening Practice (page 115)

Look at the map on page 114. Listen carefully. Where are you? Circle the letter of the correct answer.

1. You are in the front of the store, near the Entrance, next to Cosmetics. Where are you?
2. You are on the left side of the store, across from the Women's Department, next to the Photo Shop. Where are you?
3. You are in the back of the store, next to the Men's Department, and across from Jewelry. Where are you?
4. You are on the right side of the store, across from Toys, between Housewares and Automotive. Where are you?
5. You are near the Women's Department, on the right side of the store, across from Cosmetics. Where are you?

ANSWER KEY

LESSON 1

Comprehension
1. yes
2. no
3. no
4. yes
5. yes
6. no

Vocabulary / A
1. family
2. last name
3. city
4. apartment
5. hospital
6. native country
7. nervous
8. language

Vocabulary / B

```
v  c  l  a  s  j  y  c  b  o
f  i  r  s  t  p  u  o  n  e
r  t  f  g  a  s  p  u  x  d
i  y  a  d  e  e  r  n  o  u
e  s  m  a  l  o  h  t  a  c
n  e  i  g  h  b  o  r  m  a
d  o  l  a  s  t  m  y  a  t
c  r  y  n  j  a  r  s  o  i
a  m  a  r  r  i  e  d  b  o
a  p  a  r  t  m  e  n  t  n
```

Language Skills / A
1. am
2. are
3. is
4. are
5. is

1. I'm
2. They're
3. She's
4. You're
5. It's

Language Skills / B
1. Are
2. Is
3. Is
4. Is
5. Are
6. Are

Language Skills / C
1. Is he thirteen years old?
2. Are you nervous?
3. Is she a good worker?
4. Are you from El Salvador?
5. Is it Thursday?
6. Are your children in school?

LESSON 2

Comprehension
1. no
2. yes
3. no
4. yes
5. yes
6. no
7. no

Vocabulary / A
1. form
2. female
3. single
4. employer
5. male
6. signature
7. emergency
8. print

Vocabulary / B
1. area code
2. children
3. print
4. emergency
5. signature
6. address

Language Skills / A
1. am not
2. is not
3. are not
4. is not
5. is not

1. I'm not
2. isn't
3. aren't
4. isn't
5. isn't

Language Skills / B
1. No, she isn't.
2. No, I'm not.
3. No, they aren't.
4. No, it isn't.
5. No, I'm not.

More Practice: Vocabulary
1. h
2. g
3. b
4. a
5. i
6. e
7. c
8. d
9. f

LESSON 3

Comprehension
1. yes
2. no
3. no
4. yes
5. yes
6. no

Vocabulary / A

1. nationality
2. supervisor
3. departments
4. maintenance
5. housekeeping
6. laundry
7. kitchen

Vocabulary / B

1. e
2. h
3. f
4. a
5. g
6. b
7. d
8. c

Language Skills / A

1. want
2. knows
3. like

Language Skills / B

1. doesn't
2. don't
3. don't
4. doesn't

Reading Practice

1. b
2. b
3. c
4. a

More Practice: Vocabulary

1. e
2. h
3. k
4. c
5. l
6. b
7. d
8. j
9. a
10. f
11. i
12. g

LESSON 4

Comprehension

1. no
2. yes
3. yes
4. no
5. no
6. yes

Vocabulary / A

1. time card
2. supply room
3. gloves
4. hair nets
5. diet
6. cart
7. uniform
8. menu

Vocabulary / B

1. diet
2. cart
3. menu
4. measurement
5. housekeeper
6. wash

Language Skills / A

1. Do, like
2. Do, cook
3. Does, work
4. Does, wash
5. Do, need
6. Do, have
7. Does, know

More Practice: Measurement

1. 4 cups
   8 pints
   8 ounces
2. 10 cups of apples, 12 cups of peaches, 15 cups of oranges, 37 cups of fruit salad
3. 2 pints, 1 quart
4. 12 teaspoons
5. 8 quarts
6. $3\,^1/_3$ yards
7. $4\,^1/_2$ feet

Listening Practice

1. $2\,^1/_2$ qt.
2. 180 lb.
3. $^2/_3$ c.
4. 5,140 lb.
5. $3\,^3/_4$ tsp.
6. 15 gal.
7. $6\,^7/_{10}$ in.
8. 13,240 ft.

LESSON 5

Comprehension

1. yes
2. no
3. no
4. yes
5. no

Vocabulary

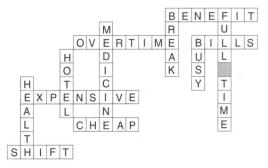

Language Skills / A

1. Can, help
2. Can, have
3. Can, work
4. Can, go
5. Can, leave

Listening Practice

1. Monday	7. September 21st
2. 6:30	8. Thursday, January 11th
3. March 30th	9. 5:15 P.M.
4. 7:45 A.M.	10. Tuesday, August 3rd
5. July 13, 2002	11. 10 past 4
6. Wednesday	12. April 19, 1996

Reading Practice

1. first
2. 30 minutes / ½ hour
3. Monday   8
   Tuesday   8
   Wednesday   8 ½
   Thursday   9
   Friday   8 ½
   Saturday   4
4. 46
5. 6

More Practice: Reading

1. b	4. c
2. c	5. b
3. c	

LESSON 6

Comprehension / A

1. yes	4. no
2. yes	5. no
3. no	6. yes

Comprehension / B

1. c	3. a
2. c	4. b

Vocabulary / A

1. storage room	4. work order
2. guest	5. inspection
3. equipment	6. elevator

Vocabulary / B

1. shelf	4. inspection
2. bathroom	5. bed
3. guest	6. tip

Language Skills

1. between
2. next to
3. above
4. below
5. behind

Listening Practice / A

1. 2	10. 1
2. 1	11. 2
3. 2	12. 2
4. 3	13. 2
5. 3	14. 1
6. 2	15. 2
7. 1	16. 3
8. 2	17. 2
9. 2	18. 3

Writing Practice / A

1. housekeeping
2. housekeeper
3. gets her work order
4. goes to the storage room and gets her cart
5. gets the supplies she needs
6.
7. } mop, cleaners, brush, paper towels, dust cloth, vacuum cleaner (any 3)
8.

LESSON 7

Comprehension / A

1. yes	4. no
2. no	5. no
3. yes	6. no

Comprehension / B

1. b	3. c
2. a	4. c

Vocabulary / A

1. holidays	4. calls in sick
2. appointment	5. cover for
3. vacation	6. unpaid

Vocabulary / B

1. problem	3. vacation
2. office	4. message

Language Skills / A

1. have
2. has
3. have
4. has
5. have

Language Skills / B

1. Do, have
2. Do, have
3. Do, have
4. Does, have
5. Does, have

Reading Practice

1. 2/25/03
2. 8:10, morning
3. She is sick.

Listening Practice / A

Date: 4/17/03
Time: 6:00 A.M.
To: Ray Jones
From: Ana Rivera
Message: Lin Wu cannot come to work today. She is sick.

Let's Think about It

Answers will vary.

LESSON 8

Comprehension / A

1. no
2. yes
3. no
4. no
5. yes

Comprehension / B

1. b
2. c
3. b
4. a

Vocabulary / A

1. pay stub
2. pay period
3. time and a half
4. earn
5. deduction
6. federal withholding tax

Vocabulary / B

1. d
2. f
3. h
4. g
5. c
6. a
7. e
8. b

Language Skills / A

1. are doing
2. are washing
3. is talking
4. are working
5. am helping

Language Skills / B

1. Is, eating
2. Are, taking
3. Is, covering
4. Are, studying

Reading Practice / B

1. 10-3-03 – 10-09-03
2. $81
3. $441
4. $37.34
5. $125.36
6. $315.64

More Practice: Reading / B

5
3
1
4
6
2

LESSON 9

Comprehension / A

1. c
2. a, b
3. b, c
4. a, c
5. a, c

Comprehension / B

1. people, teams, products, machines

Vocabulary / A

1. machines
2. team member
3. labels
4. fire alarm
5. poison
6. comfortable

Vocabulary / B

1. d
2. f
3. h
4. a
5. g
6. c
7. e
8. b

Reading Practice

1. They work at a nursing home.
2. She doesn't always understand directions. She can't read all the signs and labels.
3. No. She is afraid he will get mad.
4. She should say, "I don't understand. Can you please help me?"

LESSON 10

Comprehension / A

1. c
2. a, c
3. a
4. b
5. b, c

Comprehension / B

4
3
6
1
5
2

Vocabulary / A

1. training
2. safety rules
3. safety gear
4. mask
5. respirator
6. harmful

Vocabulary / B

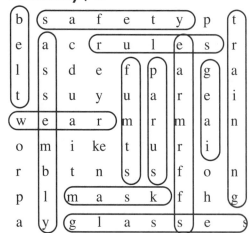

Language Skills / A

1. needed
2. helped
3. talked
4. showed

Language Skills / B

1. Did, work
2. Did, show
3. Did, wear
4. Did, get

Listening Practice / A

1. 1   7. 1
2. 1   8. 2
3. 2   9. 1
4. 2   10. 2
5. 1   11. 1
6. 2   12. 1

More Practice: Listening

1. a   3. a
2. b   4. a

LESSON 11

Comprehension / A

1. this morning
2. in the machine shop
3. George wasn't wearing gloves.

1. last week
2. in the assembly department
3. Kamel's goggles broke, and he didn't get new ones / Kamel wasn't wearing goggles.

Comprehension / B

5
2
3
6
1
4

Vocabulary / A

1. burn
2. Goggles
3. prevent
4. procedure
5. Workers' Compensation

Vocabulary / B

1. gloves
2. apron
3. first aid kit safety
4. goggles
5. boots
6. injury

Language Skills

1. did   3. put   5. took   7. went   9. made
2. was   4. broke 6. gave   8. were 10. said

Reading Practice

1. Angelo Cabral
2. in the welding department / at Goodwin Products
3. on August 16 / at 2:30 in the afternoon

Writing Practice

```
                    ACCIDENT REPORT
                     (Report of Injury)
Please print.
1. Employee Name ____Cabral_____Angelo_____
                      (Last)         (First)    (Middle Initial)
2. Department ___welding___  3. Supervisor ___Guy Le Blanc___
4. Date of Accident __August 16__  5. Time of Accident __2:30 p.m.__
6. Location of Accident ___in the welding department_____
7. How Accident Happened ___Angelo was pushing a cart. A pipe___
___fell off the cart onto his foot. He broke his foot._____

_____
8. Type of Injury (e.g., burn, cut, fracture) _____fracture_____

_____
9. Name of Person to Whom Injury Was Reported ___Guy Le Blanc___
```

LESSON 12

Comprehension / A

1. a, c
2. c
3. b, c
4. b, c
5. a, c

Comprehension / B

1. Pushpa didn't turn off the machine. She didn't tell anyone the warning light on her machine came on.
2. Boxes in front of the emergency exit, nails on the floor, a broken safety switch on a machine, the temperature on a machine is too high.
3. Bad materials and supplies make bad products.

Vocabulary

```
Q U A L I T Y   C O N T R O L
N         E         O
P         M         O
L     R E P A I R   L
U         E         S
G     T U R N   O F F
          A     P
R E P O R T     E
      S   U   B R E A K D O W N
      H   R     A
M I S T A K E   T
                E
```

Language Skills

1. had
2. saw
3. lost
4. brought
5. told
6. found
7. got
8. left
9. shut
10. got

Listening Practice

1. b
2. a
3. b
4. c
5. a

Reading Practice

1. Edna and Flor are friends. / Edna and Flor are co-workers.
2. Edna mixed ammonia and bleach together, and the fumes made her sick.
3. last week
4. Flor called 911. She talked to the dispatcher and gave him the necessary information.

LESSON 13

Comprehension / A

1. a
2. b, c
3. a
4. a, c
5. b

Comprehension / B

1. friends and neighbors
2. stores in his neighborhood and the Unemployment Office
3. bulletin boards and help wanted ads
4. applications

Vocabulary / A

1. job opening
2. application
3. temporary
4. work experience
5. wages
6. Unemployment Office

Vocabulary / B

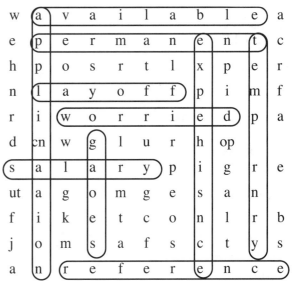

Language Skills

1. at	5. on
2. on	6. at, in
3. in	7. in
4. on	8. on, in

Reading Practice

1. Asst. Cook, Delivery Person
2. Store Clerk, Machine Operator, Laundry Worker
3. Machine Operator
4. 432-6660
5. Laura
6. Latin Village
7. Machine Operator, Laundry Worker

More Practice: Vocabulary

1. k	9. m
2. i	10. o
3. p	11. f
4. g	12. e
5. j	13. b
6. l	14. a
7. n	15. h
8. d	16. c

More Practice: Reading

1. Work has slowed down. / They lost over $3 million. / They have to close some departments.
2. He has four kids and needs a job. / There is no other place to work in the area.
3. When people are out of work, they don't spend much money.

LESSON 14

Comprehension / A

1. b, c	4. b
2. a, b	5. b, c
3. a	

Comprehension / B

1, 3, 4, 6

Vocabulary

1. deliveries
2. unload
3. stockroom
4. dolly
5. damaged
6. container
7. stock
8. prices
9. join
10. dues
11. meeting

Language Skills / A

1. next to
2. across from
3. in the back of
4. across from
5. on the left, next to
6. on the right, across from

Listening Practice

1. a
2. b
3. c
4. a
5. c

Reading Practice

1. The welfare law changed.
2. She likes to help people. / She likes to get a paycheck.
3. Luz's job makes her feel good.
4. Luz's children see her work hard, so they work hard, too.

LESSON 15

Comprehension / A

1. a, c	4. a, b
2. c	5. b, c
3. b	

Vocabulary / A

1. Customer Service
2. figure it out
3. review
4. get along with
5. raise
6. Human Resources